CREATING GOOD WORK

CREATING GOOD WORK

The World's Leading Social
Entrepreneurs Show How to
Build a Healthy Economy

Edited by
RON SCHULTZ

Foreword by
CHERYL L. DORSEY

palgrave
macmillan

CREATING GOOD WORK

First published in 2013 by
PALGRAVE MACMILLAN®
in the United States—a division of St. Martin's Press LLC,
175 Fifth Avenue, New York, NY 10010.

Where this book is distributed in the UK, Europe and the rest of the world,
this is by Palgrave Macmillan, a division of Macmillan Publishers Limited,
registered in England, company number 785998, of Houndmills,
Basingstoke, Hampshire RG21 6XS.

Palgrave Macmillan is the global academic imprint of the above companies
and has companies and representatives throughout the world.

Palgrave® and Macmillan® are registered trademarks in the United States,
the United Kingdom, Europe and other countries.

ISBN: 978–0–230–37203–0

Library of Congress Cataloging-in-Publication Data

    Creating good work : the world's leading social entrepreneurs show
how to build a healthy economy / edited by Ron Schultz; foreword
by Cheryl L. Dorsey.
        p. cm.
    Includes bibliographical references.
    ISBN 978–0–230–37203–0 (alk. paper)
    1. Social entrepreneurship. 2. Social responsibility of business.
    I. Schultz, Ron, 1951–

HD60.C74 2013
658.4′08—dc23   2012029557

A catalogue record of the book is available from the British Library.

Design by Newgen Imaging Systems (P) Ltd., Chennai, India.

First edition: February 2013

10 9 8 7 6 5 4 3 2 1

This book is dedicated to
Sam Schultz
A mench, a mentor, and my father

You've got to be very careful if you don't know where you are going, because you might not get there.

—Yogi Berra

CONTENTS

FOREWORD

Cheryl L. Dorsey
Echoing Green

RON SCHULTZ'S LATEST BOOK ARRIVES AT a critical time in the relatively short history of the social entrepreneurial movement. As Jeff Trexler points out in his perceptive chapter, despite the solid successes of many social entrepreneurs in "creating good work," the field is at something of a turning point. Critics such as *New York Times* columnist David Brooks are becoming more vocal, claiming social entrepreneurs are naïve about harsh political realities, even as large corporations threaten to co-opt the movement in the public mind by asserting that they already practice effective corporate social responsibility.

But neither government nor big business has the goal of building an enlightened society, let alone the ambition or imagination. That's the job of those special persons who want to leave the world a better place for having been here. The beauty of this book is that it gives practical, hard-won advice for how prospective and even in-the-trenches social entrepreneurs can do just that. To that end, the volume is broken down into sections that focus on theory, application, and best practices—laying out where we've come from, what we believe, and what we need to know to go forward. The last, going forward, requires constant adaptation, which is part of a good social entrepreneur's DNA.

Gregory Dees, professor of the Practice of Social Entrepreneurship and cofounder of the Center for the Advancement of Social Entrepreneurship at Duke University frames our iterating role this way: "Social entrepreneurs serve as society's 'learning laboratory,' developing, testing and refining new approaches to problems in ways that government agencies, with all their budgetary, bureaucratic, legislative, jurisdictional and political constraints, cannot do."

At Echoing Green, we constantly discover exactly this kind of pragmatic adaptation. For example, in a recent survey of our fellows in conjunction with the Harvard Business School, we saw a sharp rise in "hybrid" organizations that meld aspects of nonprofit and for-profit organizations. Over the past five years, applications from organizations that combined earned and donated revenue grew significantly: in 2010 and 2011, almost 50 percent of all applications relied on hybrid models versus 37 percent in 2006. These entrepreneurs sought to address social issues in domains as diverse as hunger, health care, economic development, environment, education, housing, culture, law, and politics.

We posit that this adaptation stems, in part, from social entrepreneurs' willingness to be less dependent on donations and subsidies, as well as from an increased interest in sustainable development solutions in the wake of the 2008 financial crisis.

One such is New York's Hot Bread Kitchen, founded by Jessamyn Rodriguez, whose mostly low-income immigrant women bake premium-priced bread inspired by their countries of origin, while learning the skills they need to integrate into the workforce and, ultimately, to achieve management track positions in the food industry. In this way, Hot Bread Kitchen combines two traditionally separate models: a social welfare model that guides its workforce development mission and a market-based model that guides its commercial activities.

This relentless search for a better way to serve humanity also gains power from what Craig Dunn, in his chapter, calls "thoughtful, caring *design* that is at the same time *deliberate* and *disruptive*, to the point of being fundamentally subversive." To more efficiently combine heart and head, Craig advocates a collaborative approach to social entrepreneurship; one that moves us beyond today's sort of hero worship of individual social entrepreneurs to almost systematize the "subversion" of the status quo. Put another way, social entrepreneurs need to do more than implement new business plans that address specific social or environmental needs with market solutions. They also must reinvent business itself as a source of shared prosperity.

That's a tall order. But the history of current-day "subversives" shows that, if nothing else, successful social entrepreneurs are persistent to the point of mania. If the reader will pardon my bias, two social entrepreneurs whose chapters stood out for me were those written by two Echoing Green Fellows—Gary Kosman, founder of America Learns, a technology platform that provides tutors of underprivileged kids with connections and resources previously unavailable to them, and Karen Tse, founder of International Bridges to Justice, which audaciously aims to eradicate torture in the twenty-first century and protect due-process rights for accused people throughout the world.

Gary relates that shortly after he started America Learns, a significant number of his tutor-providing clients simply dropped his service. The reason was cultural: nobody understood how to adequately use the technology. "Now, before we sign a contract with an organization," he says, "we walk that organization's team through an exercise that assesses their capacity to use our services well." Teamed with a "'culture integration' plan," Gary notes that his business-model changes have not only led to "near-100-percent customer retention from year to year; they've also led to faster sales cycles and far fewer customer support requests"—to say nothing of thousands more literate children.

Which gets us back to the whole history and promise of social entrepreneurship: to serve as an influential medium for integrating business and social values. Ron Schultz amusingly relates how his 12-year career as a social entrepreneur serendipitously began to form in his mind as a woman who was starting European operations for Ashoka: Innovators for the Public passed him a jar of marmalade at a London bed and breakfast. Ashoka wouldn't hire him, even after repeated attempts, but like all good social entrepreneurs, Ron found another way.

As our field matures, so also must social entrepreneurship find other ways of "creating good work." One way is by answering today's critiques, but not with counterarguments. Rather, we will do so by truly changing the way business is being done. In short, we will succeed by serving as the midwife for the emergence of a radically new conceptual framework for economic activity, one that moves from self-interested competition to organic collaboration for the benefit of the many. And this book will help build much momentum toward that goal.

ACKNOWLEDGMENTS

SINCE ONE OF THE PRIMARY LESSONS we hear throughout this book is the importance of relationships and collaboration, it is dangerous to write formal acknowledgments for the fear of leaving someone out. So, before I go about the process of naming names, let me say that I truly do appreciate the input and expertise of all and any of you who have helped me during the process of bringing this book to completion. And if perchance I fail to acknowledge you here, it is not because I don't love and appreciate you—it is simply a matter of memory.

I must begin at home. Laura Sanderford has been absolutely invaluable in helping with this process. As an exemplary teacher, she was especially helpful in identifying the lessons contained in each of the application chapters. She also kept me on track with my own writing, and when something wasn't clear to her, it would have invariably been unclear to you, the reader. Laura has also been my executive producer for years, not only producing our two remarkable daughters, but also in support of the work I have chosen to do and the challenge it often presents to such things as paying bills. Without her hard work and love, this book would not have been possible. Nor for that matter would much of the past 36 years of our life together.

This is third project on which Laurie Harting, at Palgrave Macmillian, and I have worked. As an editor, she has been true to form: her input and support has been greatly appreciated and valued. The author-editor relationship is always essential to the success of a project, and this one is no exception.

I would also like to acknowledge the support of Renee Kaplan and Sandy Herz at the Skoll Foundation, who helped me when this project was first launched to track down some of the social entrepreneurs I wanted to make sure were included and contributed. Renee was a great help early on in this process, and for that I am grateful.

Similarly in regards to early and continual support is Paul Herman (HIPInvestor). Paul was probably my first real social entrepreneurial colleague when he was with Ashoka. His help and influence on and with this project is probably greater than he realizes. Not only did Paul contribute a chapter to this compendium, but he has provided willing and gracious access whenever and wherever it was needed.

I must also mention those with whom I work closely within my own organization: Entrepreneurs4Change. That includes my good friends and colleagues, John Parsons, Dennis Washburn, and Greg Franks, president and CEO of the Tom and Ethel Bradley Foundation, under whose wing E4C currently flies. These three fellows have provided not only valued friendship, but excellent counsel and advice as I have transited these rocky shores.

From the department of "I can never acknowledge the impact of this person on my life, enough," my late colleague, friend, and mentor, Howard Sherman, requires more than mention. And everyone who knew or worked with Howard would agree that he does. It was Howard who opened me to a world of intellectual discourse and interaction that has shaped and informed every professional choice I make. The worlds of learning we explored together reached far beyond the classics and traditional resources, producing adjacent opportunities that, a decade after his passing, are still emerging.

And funny enough, if it hadn't been for my association with Howard, Todd Khozein (SecondMuse) and I would have undoubtedly remained strangers on a couch at the Skoll World Forum. But fortunately, that is not the case. Beyond our New Mexico connection and our coemergence in the world of complexity thinking and social entrepreneurship, Todd has pointed the way to the power of collaboration. He has helped me extend my ideas of relationship to manifest a whole new set of opportunities. This understanding has been invaluable in the shaping of this project.

When I first met Craig Dunn, associate dean of business at Western Washington University, while he was still a professor at San Diego State

University, I told him we were not only going to be working together, but that we would become good friends. He replied rather disdainfully, "What? In order to work with you, I have to become your friend?" A decade later, we're still friends, and I will say I have learned more about what it means to be a social entrepreneur from Craig than just about any other person around. When you read his chapter you'll know why I say that.

I would also like to express my gratitude to Mary Sue Milliken for all her help and connection, as well as to Ashoka's Beverly Schwartz, the goddess of social marketing, for whom I have tremendous respect and appreciation for challenging me along this path.

And to those who have been crucial to the development of my continuing education, allowing me to keep afloat within the two seas in which I have been swimming for the past two decades, social entrepreneurship and complexity thinking: I am grateful to the fabulous Mary Lee Rhodes, who refused to give up on me, even when she could have, my dear friend and colleague Michael Lissack, with whom I have worked on countless projects, including my last book at Palgrave Macmillan, and Jeff Goldstein, whose head and heart for combining understanding and compassion have introduced, encouraged, and supported the exploration of a grounding theory of social entrepreneurship. Thank you all.

It would not be fitting to leave Kurt Richardson out of the aforementioned group of folks who have influenced my efforts in social entrepreneurship and complexity, but that has always been an important part of our relationship, to do what is not fitting. Kurt is the publisher of Emergent Publications and the editor of the journal *E:CO*. Kurt has given me license to explore on a quarterly basis ideas that have informed and shaped the book that follows. He has offered this opportunity for years now, and the ideas in this book would never have been formulated without him.

I would also like to recognize the efforts of Josh Silberstein for his tireless support on my behalf and finally, the man we both serve, the Sakyong Mipham Rinpoche. His teaching on creating enlightened society underlies why this book is being written and how our basic goodness—our willingness to meet the world that presents itself, to be intelligent, fearless, and gentle, and to be of benefit to others—drives the work we do.

Thank you, thank you, thank you.

INTRODUCTION

Ron Schultz
Entrepreneurs4Change

WHEN MY EDITOR AT PALGRAVE MACMILLAN asked me to bring her a book on social entrepreneurship, I knew exactly what I wanted to do. I had developed a model a number of years back for what was in essence an industry bible: a compendium of the prevailing thinking and activities that describes where we came from, what we believe, and what we need to know to go forward.

Fortunately, Palgrave Macmillan agreed with my plan, and I set about the task of gathering many of the folks with whom I had worked and who I had come to know over the past dozen years of my involvement in the social entrepreneurial world. They are remarkable people, to a person. But I didn't want to produce a book about how remarkable they are. I wanted their knowledge, wisdom, and experience. I wanted a book that would be truly helpful to someone who had it in their heads that they, too, knew they were a social entrepreneur, but wanted to hear more from those who had traveled the same paths they were facing.

There were enough books in the world that had elevated these people and told great hero stories about their efforts. But there was nothing that really spoke to the practicality of getting it done. And nothing, still, that combined the personal voices of the players themselves talking about the work that was required to actualize positive change in the world and the lessons they had learned in doing so.

The model for this book is one that it is almost archetypal in its approach. It follows a path of theory, application, and practice. Theory—the ideas upon which our efforts are based; application—how we make something out of those ideas; and practice—how we develop and continue that something and move it forward.

The book is also laid out in a similar fashion, with the first section providing a theoretical understanding of why and how the work gets done, followed by stories from social entrepreneurs describing how they gave birth to the ideas that influenced their direction and work, how they turned those ideas into an enterprise, and finally what has been needed to further and continue that work.

The grounding comes first: and Craig Dunn, associate dean of business at Western Washington University, in Bellingham WA, introduces a rather extraordinary definition and description of what social entrepreneurship is all about—"Deliberate Disruptive Design." He lays out the historical context as only a practitioner and academician can. This chapter sets our thematic tone of what drives a social entrepreneur, how the work gets done, and why it's not just more of the same. From this base of understanding unfolds an amazing continuum of personal path, collaborative accomplishment, social understanding, and pertinent lessons.

One of the personal benefits of putting together a volume like this is that I got to read these pieces before anyone else. I admit that I am not a partial observer, but all I did was put an idea out into the world and people I knew delivered what they knew at a level from which everyone benefits. Craig Dunn's redefining of the social entrepreneurial world and experience will shift thinking and perceptions for years to come.

But now, once you've assimilated Dunn's ideas, hold on to your hats, because what Jeff Trexler then adds to the perspective of social entrepreneurship is sure to blow off a number of people's heads. In "Understanding Social Enterprise," Trexler takes his long and deep understanding of the field of social entrepreneurship and his experience outside of it to challenge social entrepreneurs to do exactly what Dunn has said we must do with our social challenges—but do so to our own industry: continually apply the idea of deliberate disruptive design to our own work. As we have tended to glorify the successes within the social entrepreneurial world,

Trexler makes the case that we cannot ignore those who challenge it. For the ideals of social entrepreneurship to have the impact we perceive it to have, we must be willing to look at the warts, too. Two of the essential roles of leadership are to repeat the message over and over and emulate the behavior you want others to follow. If we are truly dedicated to creating a social entrepreneurial world that makes a positive difference, and affects the kinds of change we want to see, we have to blow up the pedestal on which social entrepreneurs have been placed, and be willing to disrupt the limitations of our own thinking.

My contribution follows Trexler's. And it discusses "Why Change Happens and Why it Sometimes Doesn't." I have spent the greater part of the last three decades looking at this notion of change. It began with a seven-month conversation I had with Nobel physicist Murray Gell-Mann, who theorized the existence and named the fundamental particle of the atom, the quark. I came to Murray to do a four-day interview for *Omni Magazine*, with the mistaken notion that somewhere in the fundamental particle of the atom, the essence of creativity must lie. Murray told me in the first 20 minutes of our meeting I was wrong and everything I thought was wrong. "You can't build those bridges," he said. "Talk to the Complex Adaptive Systems scientists." Seven month later, when the interview was finally completed, I had become a complex adaptive systems junkie. Of course, Murray already was one, too. Complex Adaptive Systems (human beings being one iteration) are all about how change happens and new things emerge. Bringing this thinking into the realm of social entrepreneurship in a way that it could not only be understood but utilized has been what's driven my work. "Why Change Happens" takes the reader through what I have found to be the most useful methodology for shifting intransigence and connecting it to the work of social entrepreneurs.

In his chapter "Legal Issues for Social Entrepreneurship," Allen Bromberger, undoubtedly the leading legal voice in the social business world, provides a detailed account of what every social entrepreneur had better be aware of, unless they want to spend a great deal of time and money in the judicial system. You might think that as a social entrepreneur you can leave the legal issues to the lawyers, but you would be wrong. This definitive voice lays out the rules in a fashion that further distinguishes the social entrepreneurial model from traditional business and charities. The rules may not be as exciting as the playing field, but if you try playing the game without them, one thing is certain: You're going to lose.

Once we understand why and how we've entered this realm of enterprising service, and how to do so legally, it becomes of even greater importance that we know how to get the word out about the efforts we make, so that we can serve our greater markets and create resources that will support those efforts. Alan Andreason, provides an expert analysis of the particular form of marketing that has come into being to support social enterprise and social business. Not too surprisingly, it's called "social marketing." I have met very few marketing people who won't tell you that every form of business is marketing. Operations, mission, finances, and legal issues aside, telling the compelling story is certainly the means to engage others throughout the enterprise chain. One of the great social marketers of our time, Phil Harvey, recognized early on that the way to decrease an out-of-control population growth in developing nations was to increase the use of condoms. His campaigns throughout Asia and Africa resulted in saving thousands of lives and preventing an epidemic of overpopulation. The strength of the program was solely one of marketing the message again and again. And as Harvey points out in his groundbreaking book *Let Every Child Be Wanted* (Auburn House, 2002), it was Alan Andreason who provided the definitive definition of the power of this opportunity— "to influence the voluntary behavior of target audiences to improve their personal welfare and that of society of which they are a part."

Getting the word out about the work being done to shift long-entrenched social ailments is indeed an essential piece in the social entrepreneurial puzzle. Making sure outcomes are being realized and the desired impact is being achieved has become a hallmark characteristic required to ensure investment and resource in social businesses. The challenge has always been one of trying to quantify human suffering and its relief and to make sure what we have said we want to accomplish is actually getting done. In the area of metrics and evaluation, we provide two interlinked chapters by R. Paul Herman, founder and president of the HIPInvestor and Glenda Eoyang, whose organization, Human Dynamic Systems, looks at the underlying interactions that produce action and how we capture what emerges. In Paul Herman's work, he details how it is possible to not only do *good*, but to do well by doing good. Paul's work in establishing a social impact scorecard to be applied to all business enterprises, and from that an index of profitable indicators, is revolutionizing how corporations, large and small, and social businesses measure their own outcomes so they can not only produce profit for stockholders and stakeholders, but demonstrate how their work is benefiting their communities and society as a whole.

But when dealing with the human impact of social entrepreneurs, metrics are only part of the equation. As Glenda Eoyang makes clear in her chapter titled "Evaluating Complex Change" there is useful evaluation, and then there is the feedback that can lead one down a rat hole of useless information. Characterizing change as anything other than complex is to miss the fundamental understanding of how change emerges out of the interactions of the players involved. Because complex emergence is not predictable, we cannot expect the same sort of industrial strength measurement techniques that drive a factory output to deliver a useful reflection of the impact of human interaction. What emerges out of the interactions of complex living systems, of which we humans are a part, simply defies a linear progression. It is based on several previous interactions that an individual may have experienced and when you combine that with others with as equally a diverse chain of experience, it is impossible to predict what will emerge. Fortunately, even though we cannot predict that by initiating this interaction we will get this result, we can explain what arises in a fashion that we can point directly to outcomes that have emerged. Glenda's work is about being able to capture what emerges out of these complex iterations and demonstrate the impact and shift that has taken place. For funders and supporters this, together with traditional metrics, provides a much more complete picture of impact and measurement than numbers alone. And with this chapter we close our theoretical discussion of the grounding ideas upon which the social entrepreneurial enterprises we launch are founded.

What follows, introduced section by section, are the practitioners at work. How they have taken these ideas and turned them into a something—an enterprise that is challenging business-as-usual at every turn and having a profound impact on how life on this planet shows up. While the stories of the social entrepreneurs are compelling and moving, it is how they meet their challenges that is of real use here. And as will become evident as you read through the application chapters, each of these social entrepreneurs has employed his or her own particular form of deliberate disruptive design to blow up the old models, rules, and behaviors that have governed how we help each other. Social entrepreneurship is not about *us* helping *them*—it is our recognition that we are all in this together and that any real solution can only arise from the development of our interdependence and our working together to create good work.

Section 1

LAYING THE THEORETICAL FOUNDATIONS FOR SOCIAL ENTREPRENEURSHIP

Chapter 1

DELIBERATE DISRUPTIVE DESIGN

Craig P. Dunn
Associate Dean of Business,
Western Washington University

While its roots are deep in our past, over the last three decades we have witnessed an explosion of innovation as a growing international community of individuals has experimented with a great variety of approaches to fulfilling one basic idea:

Markets and business, capital and commerce can be harnessed not simply for the creation of individual wealth, but rather the creation of value in its fullest.

—Jed Emerson, Foreword, *Social Enterprise Typology*
(emphasis in the original)

SOCIAL ENTREPRENEURSHIP IS A RAPIDLY shifting field ranging from the work of philosophers to that of economists to that of organizational theorists to that of social scientists to that of philanthropists to perhaps the most vital aspect, the work of ordinary folk seeking simply to leave the world a better place than they found it. The term "social entrepreneurship," however, fails to adequately capture both the *head* and the *heart* of the matter: thoughtful, caring *design* that is at the same time *deliberate* and *disruptive*, to the point of being fundamentally subversive.

Before probing the heart of social entrepreneurship, how might the mounting literature on social entrepreneurship be meaningfully organized? Perhaps it would be best to step back for a moment and consider the grounding for knowledge, which is: What is truth? And, how do we access truth? These are two of the most essential questions facing us as we strive to make sense of the world in which we find ourselves—and answers are particularly vital with respect to emerging topics such as social entrepreneurship.

Those trained at virtually any institution of higher education come to appreciate evidence-based, empirical research conducted against the backdrop of very exacting assumptions. It is assumed, for example, that there exists an objective reality apart from the observer. This reality is there to be discovered, and the *process* of discovery does not impact the truth itself. Knowledge accumulates in a regimented iterative cycle of conjecture. This leads to the development of a hypothesis, which in turn leads to hypothesis testing, and then to interpretation of the findings, which leads back to modification of the original conjecture and further hypothesis development, testing, and further interpretation of findings, ad infinitum. Through this progression we come to a better understanding of the world in which we live—if not of our place in that world.

We seem naturally driven to reinforce an orderly understanding of the universe. The scientific method just described nets an enormous volume of evidence that needs to be organized in some logical fashion. To that end, we engage in a variety of tactics. One is to draw similarities and distinctions: In what ways is social entrepreneurship *similar* to traditional entrepreneurship? In what ways is social entrepreneurship *dissimilar* to traditional entrepreneurship? It has been argued that the centrality of the social mission contributes to the distinction between social entrepreneurship and other forms of entrepreneurship.[1]

A second organizational tactic is to categorize: Social entrepreneurship ranges along a continuum of *for-profit* to *not-for-profit* enterprise and along a continuum of *social goals* to *commercial exchange*. One such approach has been to delineate the salient legal distinctions that differentiate organizational forms, providing within each several examples of social entrepreneurial activity.[2] However, while theorists and practitioners alike have generally moved well beyond the narrow view that "[s]ocial enterprise refers to non-profits that operate businesses both to raise revenue and to further the social missions of their organizations,"[3] a quick literature search uncovers a glut of claims that social entrepreneurship is solidly and exclusively grounded in the not-for-profit sector of the larger economy.

A third is to differentiate individual behavior from organizational behavior: What are the *characteristics* of a *successful* social entrepreneur? What are the *effective tactics* employed by social entrepreneurs? Several successful entrepreneurial methods have been outlined and categorized as harmonizing strategies, deisolating strategies, and leadership strategies.[4]

A fourth is to establish hierarchy: "*[S]ocial entrepreneurs are one species in the genus entrepreneur.*"[5] This oft-quoted statement by one of the prominent forces in entrepreneurship implies a subservient role for social entrepreneurship within the broader field in which it is presumed to reside.

A fifth is to expose the antecedents of a process: Is social entrepreneurship a *response* to *market failure*? How are *intentions* to create a social enterprise *formed*? In a macro sense, "future entrepreneurs will likely be more socially concerned than those of the past—not necessarily as a result of their own value orientations but as a response to an evolution of thought regarding the social responsibility of business activity in general."[6] This general statement comes on the heels of numerous more specific claims, such as the one that "social entrepreneurship has a distinct mission: to combat market failures aggravated by disenfranchisement,"[7] with arguments here situated on mitigating the negative externalities that often attend the operation of unconstrained markets.

A sixth is to evaluate the performance of social entrepreneurial ventures: How should one *assess organizational effectiveness*? Nonempiricists suggest that performance measurement needs to rely on more than qualitative, case-based research, and advocate for employing the rigors of double-bottom-line or triple-bottom-line analysis.[8]

But something beyond developing categorization schemes is needed in order to understand the underlying social entrepreneurship construct. Three methods extend existing knowledge to draw conclusions or construct explanations: *inductive reasoning, deductive reasoning,* and *abductive reasoning.* Inductive reasoning maintains we know social entrepreneurship when we see it, and that its general principles can be inferred from observation of cases describing specific instances of social entrepreneurship. Much of the current manuscript offers the reader the opportunity to draw conclusions about social entrepreneurship *writ large* from rich description of particular exemplars. Although such inductive inferences are not logical necessities, they nonetheless amplify knowledge. Alternatively, deductive reasoning was employed earlier in the chapter to show how empirical literature, related to social entrepreneurship, was analytically organized. The reader will now be invited to engage in a thought experiment serving to deconstruct the term "social entrepreneurship," which will prove an exercise in abductive reasoning, "characterized by a lack of completeness, either in evidence, or in the explanation, or both"—a process that can be creative, intuitive, or even revolutionary.[9]

JARRING JUXTAPOSITIONS

So much critical research for such a young field! But the question that arises is: Is "social entrepreneurship" even the right term to describe the topic under investigation? Or alternatively framed: Is the *head* sufficient to frame the field of social entrepreneurship, or is the *heart* necessary as well? In order to answer this question, let's begin with Immanuel Kant's categorical imperative, summarized as the universal requirement that natural persons be treated as something other than mere *means* to some further *end.* Kant's demand is grounded in a fundamental commitment to the inherent dignity and liberty of the individual.

But Kant's categorical imperative is consistently and unreflectively violated in the dogged usage of certain common business expressions. Consider the phrase "human resource management." If one pays even cursory attention to this conjoining of words, one cannot escape the exclusive focus placed on prizing persons *only* for their *utility*, rather than for their intrinsic value. Humans—as with land and capital in the economist's parlance—are on this turn of phrase valued merely for what they can produce. To the extent humans are valued only for their productive capacity, however, they are *undervalued*. And while this usage has worked its way into the very fabric of virtually every business organization, the damage done does not stop here: many are now unabashedly fond of referring to real, living, purpose-driven individuals as "human assets" and "human capital."

What is striking about each of these phrases is that they share in common a fusing of the *sacred* and the *economic*. Humanity itself is a sacred idea, capturing as it does fundamental notions of nobility and purpose and choice. Economics, on the other hand, has been referred to as the "dismal science" for over a century and a half now.

There persist other—and better—examples of what should be recognized as jarring juxtapositions, but that are accepted as if they actually mean something. Consider the practice of *exchanging gifts*. Really? What can that possibly mean? The idea of *exchange* is the cornerstone of economic theory and references the act of giving something with every expectation of getting in return something of equal or greater value—else why would one engage in the exchange? The idea of *gift* is sacred and indicates the act of giving something with no expectation of getting something in return. There is a difference between exchange and gift, and we know it. If a gift is given, and the gift-giver awaits a gift in return, then the alleged act of gift-giving was not that at all. And if the hoped-for reciprocity never materializes, the gift-giver should not cling to the claim that the act was gift; rather, an honest assessment would have this act considered an *unfulfilled* exchange. Conversely, if the impulse of a gift-receiver is to reciprocate with a gift out of some sense of felt obligation to generate cosmic fairness, the recipient has diminished the sacred quality of the gift by seeking to convert it into an exchange.

What does this have to do with *social entrepreneurship*? Here is the rub. The idea of being *social* is sacred. To a great extent our core personal identities are formed and understood in relation to the other, while what it means to be moral is summed up by how we treat others. On the other hand, the idea of entrepreneurship has existed for over two centuries and has always referenced innovative market-based activity carried out against the backdrop of *economic*—particularly capitalistic—ideals and principles. There you have it: the confounding of the sacred and the economic. To return to the abbreviated literature review mentioned earlier, the purely *scientific* study of social enterprise depends entirely on the reasonableness of uniting the sacred and the economic. Furthermore, such analytic inquiry privileges the head over the heart—and the spirit.

AN ALTERNATE CONCEPTUALIZATION

As considered earlier, the scientific method seems at the same time *objective, rational,* and *rigorous.* Inquiry into the sociology of science calls into question such assumptions, oftentimes going so far as to suggest that "the construction of facts…is a *collective* process"—with the accompanying implication that truth is a *social construction* of reality rather than *objective* reality.[10]

In the process of truth discovery, it is easy to work from what we know and modify that knowledge as we go along. We know something about entrepreneurship; we can bring considerations of social justice to this construct and end up with some understanding of social entrepreneurship. This approach has produced findings that are consistent with the demands of science, and at the same time are expedient. But accurate? What if the construct called for is *entirely new,* rather than a modification to or extension of existing knowledge?

There are at least three dimensions of what has come to be known as social entrepreneurship that ought to be given attention. First the activity is *deliberate.* We are familiar with the notion that evolution takes place as random variations in nature are retained due to their improved environmental fit. Part of what is distinctive about human activity is our ability to engage in *deliberate* rather than random choice and behavior. Considered adaptive shifts in response to system changes support the view that "social enterprise is an algorithm rather than a particular kind of organization, with a specific set of traits or a prescribed mission."[11] This intentionality is essential to the activity that has come to be known as social entrepreneurship.

The second dimension is *disruption*, as understood in contrast to incremental change. At least three perspectives have been referenced within discussions of disruptive innovation: radical *product, technology,* and *business-model* development.[12] It has been argued that each of these disruptions arises in a different way, posing different competitive advantages, and requiring disparate responses from its incumbents. Whatever form it takes, such disruption is essential to social entrepreneurship.

The final dimension is *design*—not as a "downstream step in the development process" but rather as innovative systems thinking serving to unite *inspiration, ideation,* and *implementation,*[13] crossing the traditional boundaries between public, for-profit, and not-for-profit enterprises. Inspiration comes from the practice of embedding oneself in the lives of the people one is designing for,[14] and oftentimes involves *positive deviance*—looking for solutions among the ranks of those who are already doing well. Meaningful field research is a process of synthesis that leads to change. Consistent with disruptive innovation, such change is not obvious and incremental, but rather a result of divergent thinking. The final stage of design is to translate the best ideas into concrete action plans, allowing for rapid prototyping as a way of identifying unforeseen implementation challenges and unintended consequences.[15] Design thinking, involving the three aspects of inspiration, ideation, and implementation, is essential to social entrepreneurship.

In essence, social entrepreneurship is *deliberate disruptive design.* This formulation is liberating in that it extends the construct beyond the bounds of traditional entrepreneurship—and empirical science— and in so doing stimulates new opportunities for creative and economic undertakings in the service of social justice. In short, it engages the heart. Moreover, the concept of deliberate disruptive design dodges the conflation of sacred and economic terms, which is unavoidable when referring to social entrepreneurship.

But what of the initial claim that deliberate disruptive design is fundamentally subversive?

Deliberative disruptive design is meant to address persistent problems. Such problems, many having to do with social inequities, are seldom resolved through traditional economic means—rather, they tend to be exacerbated by such means. "These problems all have people at their heart… [t]hey require a human-centered, creative, iterative and practical approach to finding the best ideas and ultimate solutions."[16] Given the escalation of social inequities within pure market systems, the system itself needs to be overturned (not abandoned), for complete change to take place—that is, it needs to be subverted. Deliberate disruptive design bears the potential to harness that which is effective within market systems (the *head*) as a legitimate means to attaining greater social justice (the *heart*).

NOTES

1. Nicholis & Cho (2008), among many others, offer this argument.
2. See, e.g., Schaeffer & Dunn (2008).
3. http://www.community-wealth.org.
4. See, e.g., Khanin (2011).
5. Dees (1998); emphasis in the original.
6. Dunn & Schaeffer (2008).
7. Khanin (2011).
8. See, e.g., Schaeffer & Dunn (2008).
9. Deductive, inductive, and abductive reasoning—TIP Sheet, Butte College.
10. For a seminal reference in this regard, consider Latour (1987); emphasis in the original.
11. Trexler (2009), as referenced in Swanson & Zhang (2011).
12. Markides (2006).
13. Brown (2008).
14. Brown & Wyatt (2010).
15. Ibid.
16. Brown (2008).

REFERENCES CITED

Brown, T. (2008) "Design thinking." *Harvard Business Review*, June.

Brown, T., & J. Wyatt. (2010) "Design thinking for social innovation." *Stanford Social Innovation Review*, pp. 31–35.

Dees, J. G. (1998) "The meaning of 'social entrepreneurship.'" Stanford University: Draft Report for the Kauffman Center for Entrepreneurial Leadership, 6 pp.

Dunn, C. P., & L. Schaeffer. (2008) "Ethics of entrepreneurship." In Robert W. Kolb (ed.), *Encyclopedia of Business Ethics and Society*. Thousand Oaks, CA: Sage Publications, vol. 2: pp. 724–728.

Khanin, Dmitry. (2011) "Market failures and the strategies of social entrepreneurship." *Academy of Management Paper Proceedings*.

Latour, B. (1987) *Science in Action: How to Follow Scientists and Engineers through Society*. Harvard, MA: Harvard University Press.

Markides, C. (2006) "Disruptive innovation: In need of better theory." *Journal of Product Innovation Management*, 23: 19–25.

Nicholis, A., & A. H. Cho. (2008) "Social entrepreneurship: The structuration of a field." In A. Nicholls (ed.), *Social Entrepreneurship: New Models of Sustainable Social Change*. New York: Oxford University Press, pp. 99–118.

Schaeffer, L., & C. P. Dunn. (2008) "Social entrepreneurship." In Robert W. Kolb (ed.), *Encyclopedia of Business Ethics and Society*. Thousand Oaks, CA: Sage Publications, vol. 4: pp. 1963–1968.

"Social Enterprise." *Community-Wealth.org: A Project of the Democracy Collaborative at the University of Maryland*: http://www.community-wealth.org/strategies/panel /social/index.html.

Swanson, L. A., & D. D. Zhang. (2011) "Complexity theory and the social entrepreneurship zone." *E:CO* vol. 13, no. 3.

Trexler, J. (2009) "Social entrepreneurship as an algorithm: Is social enterprise sustainable?" In J. A. Goldstein, J. K. Hazy, and J. Silberstang (eds.), *Complexity Science and Social Entrepreneurship: Adding Social Value through Systems Thinking*. Litchfield Park, AZ: ISCE Publishing, pp. 43–69.

Chapter 2

UNDERSTANDING SOCIAL ENTERPRISE

Jeff Trexler
Second Tree Ventures

I NEVER SET OUT TO BE a social entrepreneur.

When I started my career as an attorney and consultant, the most prominent meme among those working for social change was civil society. The collapse of Soviet communism seemed to have ushered in a democratic golden age, for which nonprofit NGOs would provide the social capital necessary for robust governments and markets.

Within less than a decade, everything changed.

In Russia, where I helped write new laws on charity and social organizations, nonprofits rapidly lost public trust. A substantial contribution to this problem was their sudden use of business activity to fund their work, a practice that gave rise to suspicion and disgust in a country where they were known as *nekommercheskii*, or noncommercial, organizations. By the turn of the new millennium, the Russian government had co-opted the concept of civil society and was on its way to making nonprofits an arm of the state.

A somewhat different turn of events had taken place in the West, particularly in the United States and other countries spearheading a new technological revolution. The claim that nonprofits were the heart of innovation and social benefit seemed increasingly inconsistent with an entrepreneurial culture that was changing the world. The millennial vision of civil society quickly gave way to the promotion of venture philanthropy and social entrepreneurship, with so-called traditional grant-funded nonprofits dismissed as inefficient and ineffective.

Experiencing these seismic shifts in the social realm transformed my understanding of business and the pursuit of social good. My own suspicions of corporate enterprise were tempered by a new appreciation of its potential for improving society in ways that could equal, if not exceed, organized charity, and I also worked with a number of nonprofits engaged in cutting-edge commerce and finance.

At the same time, the marginalization of civil society in Russia and the West gave me new perspectives on institutional development. I had opposed the commercialization of Russian nonprofits because of the rhetorical disconnect, but viewing that experience in light of public regard for the entrepreneurs in computing and communications led me to study how businesses could persuade people to see profit-seeking activity as something more. The lesson from Russia was not that nonprofits should resist commercializing, but rather that they need to be strategic in identity design.

FROM TIPPING POINT TO TURNING POINT

Analogous to civil society at the height of the democratic revolutions of the early 1990s, a decade later social enterprise thrived in a symbiotic relationship with tech companies, the financial industry, and consulting services such as McKinsey and Bain. Remaking charity as a socially conscious business venture gave advocates of social enterprise a decided market advantage, particularly among young people and executives. It associated social entrepreneurs with the wellsprings of growth and innovation, provided business leaders with a form of philanthropy that seemed like an extension of themselves, and implicitly relegated those outside the movement to a swiftly fading past.

Enhancing the robustness of social entrepreneurship was the capacity for its programmatic identity—the integration of entrepreneurial and socially constructive values—to take shape in a rich array of forms. For some, the concept refers to nonprofit organizations applying more efficient methods to produce measurable impact. Others extend the concept to include socially responsible commercial business, maximizing not just shareholder wealth but social benefit and environmental sustainability in pursuit of a triple bottom line. And these are far from the only expressions of the hybridizing principle. Social entrepreneurship can equally refer to disruptive innovation that creates new solutions to seemingly intractable problems or egalitarian worker cooperatives that have been embodying this principle for decades.

While the network of ideas and entities blending entrepreneurship and social benefit continued to expand throughout the mid-2000s, its very success helped foster an insensitivity to design that made it vulnerable in the long term. It may seem hard to believe, but just five years ago a book such as the one you hold in your hands now would have touted investment banks and mortgage-backed securities as models for innovative philanthropy.

The shift was perhaps most telling in the emergence of a new vocabulary for doing good. Within the social enterprise network, words adapted from business displaced language that had served to distinguish other-directedness as an identity beyond commerce and finance. Impact investing, start-ups, ventures, social ROI, social capital markets, charitable giving portfolios, metrics, efficiency, going to scale—social enterprise became a wonderland of Wall Street buzzwords, each one reinforcing the impression that charity was no longer a space apart from an increasingly commodified society.

So long as entrepreneurship seemed like the sure path to success, raising questions about such developments seemed out of step with the times. One noteworthy example of this is the overwhelmingly negative response to SeedCo's *The Limits of Social Enterprise*, a 2007 case study of a failed child-care venture. Proponents of social entrepreneurship savaged what was in fact a rather thoughtful and tempered reflection. "Social enterprise is hot enough that entrenched players...are starting to attack the concept," a typical observer charged; "[p]eople entrenched by the status quo are threatened by new ideas as they gain momentum." Thus the movement descended into groupthink—social entrepreneurs may have called for others to rethink their activity, but they saw no need to apply the same self-critique to themselves.

A year later the momentum reversed. Business rhetoric and revenue-generating activity went from "hot" to suspect literally overnight, as the economic collapse of 2008 raised serious questions about the fundamental soundness of business practices. The poor economy also changed the valence of social good rebranded as a business. For nonprofits, profiting from the poor and talking like investment bankers stood out in sharper contrast that just a year before, especially when compared to how for-profit businesses were remaking their own brand. To shore up trust and to get people back to buying, commercial branding at times made business sound more charitable than charities themselves.

While social enterprise seemed to be poised to remake philanthropy and commercial business, it is now at a historical turning point. Social entrepreneurship still continues as a meme and movement; if it lives up to its own rhetoric by taking a rigorous and radical new look at itself, it can rise above the challenges posed by recent social and economic shifts. However, it also faces the all too real possibility of being co-opted and marginalized in a manner akin to that of civil society.

Signs of marginalization are already evident in the media and among nonprofits. Critiques of social enterprise have become more vocal and less sympathetic, and even social entrepreneurs are beginning to talk about the instructive value of failure and the strategic benefit of grants.

A more counterproductive development within social enterprise has been the movement's splintering as groups try to adapt. Differences that may have once seemed academic suddenly become important at a time when resources are scarce. Some groups are doubling down on self-sustaining commerce as a sine qua non of true social enterprise, but others are pulling back from revenue generation to emphasize measurement or changemaking instead. There has also been noteworthy fracturing along ideological lines, such as the recent split between Fair Trade USA and Fair Trade International over accommodation to industry in defining ethical business.

Apparent successes are likewise posing their own challenges. For example, the conspicuous integration of corporate social responsibility into commercial marketing has raised the specter of greenwashing, the use of environmental and other claims without a substantial basis. A more subtle challenge is surfacing as an unintended consequence of legal reform aimed at creating new legal entities, such as the benefit corporation and the L3C, that blend profit generation with social purposes. Although these new forms have the potential to provide discrete benefits in regard to branding and fiduciary responsibility, they also implicitly concede that social benefit does not have a place in standard commercial businesses.

Further increasing the risk of a marginal shift is the recent appropriation of the terms "social enterprise" and "social business" by the IT industry. Leveraging the goodwill associated with these concepts, Salesforce and other companies are using viral marketing to make these phrases synonymous with the use of online social media within a corporate infrastructure. If this usage continues to hold, the notion that social enterprise serves the common good will no doubt indeed persist, but only with the bounded network of those committed to the cause.

CORPORATE LIFE AND PERSONAL VALUES

Whatever its implications for the future of social entrepreneurship as a form of doing good, the relatively rapid dissemination of social enterprise and social business as terms associated with the use of social media highlights the value of a familiar semantic anchor. Practically everyone in a business or nonprofit organization has at least heard of online social media, so extending this to communication within the firm seems only natural. The notion of social enterprise as some kind of blended value venture, though, can take some explanation for people not already familiar with the movement, and even those within it continue to debate precisely what it means.

The first is the use of the term "social enterprise" to refer to the joint-stock company, a for-profit corporation owned by multiple shareholders. The source: none other than Karl Marx, who in *Das Kapital* argued that the social enterprise, owned by one group of individuals and managed by another, represented a key transitional form from a wholly private company to a company owned and controlled by the workers within a communist society. This use of social enterprise entered Soviet law, where for decades it stood for worker-controlled, as opposed to state-run, companies producing for themselves and for the communal good.

The term migrated into capitalist countries in the early 1980s, when the Solidarity labor union in Communist Poland used Soviet law against the state to counter government repression. Solidarity's advocacy for nongovernmental social enterprise as a democratically managed and socially beneficial corporate ideal went global, and it did not take for progressively minded Westerners to assert that social enterprise could serve as a model for capitalism as well. Except there was one important difference—lacking an anchor in Western law, the form became a medium for expressing any number of approaches to integrating entrepreneurial and social values.

Does this leap from Soviet shipyards to Wall Street shipyards mean that the first social entrepreneurs in the United States were just a sneaky bunch of left-wing communists? Not at all. Bill Drayton was working at the business consulting stalwart McKinsey when he gave life to the social enterprise model in Ashoka, and like most if not all other Westerners unschooled in Soviet law, he would have had no reason to see the idea as anything but an attempt to reform the Marxist-Leninist regime. What made the social enterprise model seem so naturally universal was that it expressed an insight that had been associated with the concept back at its beginnings, as a way of referring to the corporation as a legal form. When people join together in a group that has a shared identity, they are not just using a social medium to get business done. They have become a part of something that is greater than themselves.

The difference between the two main rival understandings of social enterprise points to a broader and more problematic rift within current corporate life. The newer version emerging out of Web 2.0, which sees social enterprise as people using online social media to communicate more effectively within a venture, sees organizational technology as fundamentally a neutral tool. We bring our goals to our work and cooperate to make things happen, whether making lots of money, doing social good, or some combination of both. The social good understanding of social enterprise, intuitively if not theoretically, sees the organic yet distinct relation between connected individuals within a bigger whole, as an organization that both expresses and shapes our ethical perspective in profound ways.

Social enterprise can still fulfill its early promise of serving as an influential medium for integrating business and social values. However, to accomplish this we need a more comprehensive understanding of how it functions as an ethical technology. In this regard there are two central issues: how social enterprise provides a medium for defining individual and corporate identity, and how this relates to the existing nonprofit and for-profit forms that, in practice, anchor them in working life.

In regard to the individual sense of self, consider the references to impact and change that recur through all forms of social enterprise. Worldchanging, metrics, forging a new equilibrium, solving intractable problems, The Girl Effect, DoSomething.org—there is much more going on here than simply making the good more businesslike. Part of the root appeal of social enterprise is that it defines individuals as people who make things happen. Whether the results actually live up to the branding is, for our present purpose, beside the point; what is significant is that the movement provides its adherents with a sense of personal agency.

Establishing one's capacity to act and to produce discrete effects is a premium value at a time when people have a heightened yet all too overwhelming awareness of networks and complex systems. We often hear that the Internet and social media give individuals an unprecedented level of control, but the same tools that give us levers of control can also make us painfully aware of how little influence we have. In a world marked by global social networks and systemic social problems, social entrepreneurship provides a way for people to link themselves to something that measurably acts. They are changemakers. They can do things. They can show what they have done.

The socially beneficial nature of this personal agency is equally important. Beyond the simple act of making something happen, social enterprise appeals to the quintessentially human desire to transform the given elements and conditions of existence into something more. In the mythology of social entrepreneurship, a so-called traditional nonprofit leaves individuals in a mundane position where they do not create—they just accept what they are given; wash, rinse, and repeat. Mainstream for-profit business ostensibly improves on this by creating new things that have value, but for social enterprise this too has its limits. By operating solely to maximize the wealth of shareholders, a for-profit business does not rise above itself.

By contrast, social entrepreneurs create an identity where they can do well by doing good. Couched in imported business buzzwords this can at times ring false, but it is ethical in the fullest sense of the word. In the original Greek, ethics was a form of persuasion, the expression of choices through which we convince ourselves and others that our lives transcend self-directed satisfaction of reductionistic material drives. We do not simply eat, reproduce, and get all we can with no regard for others; self-constraint and transformation make us what we are. In this regard the integrated identity propagated by social entrepreneurship is one that is ethically whole. We do not have to split our lives in two, doing whatever we must to get money in business while setting aside a separate time for looking beyond ourselves.

Offering hope for a meaningful existence may not be unique to social entrepreneurship, but it is quintessentially human. People put on social enterprise in much the same way they put on ethical fashion—it is not merely utilitarian; it helps create and express who they are. This identity-mediating aspect of social enterprise also helps explain why the movement has such a strong appeal for the young, from teenagers to twenty-somethings launching their careers. The customary you-children-are-our-future paeans to the exemplary commitment of young people often heard at social enterprise gatherings misses the real reason they are there. At a point in life when identity formation is foremost on their minds, social enterprise speaks to their existential anxiety. They may be leaving home and school to face life on their own, but they do not want to lose themselves in need and soulless work.

If the only value of social entrepreneurship were the holding out of hope, we might be tempted to say that it is little more than a do-gooder Honest John selling naïve Pinocchio the dream of a meaningful life, while leaving him to toil on Donkey Island. Yet social enterprise also blends its idealistic vision with one that is also pragmatic, even if not always expressed in the most strategic ways.

Social enterprise may no longer be synonymous with the shareholder-owned corporation, yet this resonance with our personal sense of self nonetheless provides an intuitive link with corporate identity in all its forms, from the ones we find in law to the expression of identity in branding. Just as each of us is more than the sum of our cells, bodily functions, and physical drives, corporate identity is only coherent when you cannot reduce it to just individuals and money. This defining ratio of difference between self and substance is the root of ethical reasoning for the individual is thus the root of our corporate life as well.

The transformative phenomenon that gives corporate form its meaning is known in scientific circles as "emergence," the appearance of integrated properties distinct from their constituent parts. In nature and in many groups, emergence is spontaneous, but corporate form was programmed to create an image of emergent identity as its defining trait. In much the same way that social enterprise takes shape in widely different ways, there is a continuum of corporate identity: for-profit corporations arguably project the lowest degree of transformation; charities, the highest. Nonetheless, even the for-profit corporation has legally mandated ethical constraints designed to keep self-interest in check.

It is precisely here that social entrepreneurship can play a vital role. The maximization of shareholder wealth at all costs has all but erased the sense that a for-profit corporation has a unified identity that is greater than its constituent parts. Similarly, nonprofits and charities have substantially lost sight of their own design logic, which can lead to both an unsustainable neglect of economic strategy and an unartful use of business that can undermine public trust. As a medium exemplifying the integration of finance and transformation, social enterprise has the potential to serve as a model for maintaining coherence in all forms of corporate identity.

EVERYTHING THAT RISES MUST CONVERGE

Social enterprise has evolved into a concept that transcends any single tactic, as its chief value lies in mediating ethical expressions of individual and

corporate identity. The opportunities this creates for making a real difference are too numerous to mention. One may not actually be able literally
to change the entire world by eliminating systemic problems that defy a
glib solution, but every possible point of contact with a business venture,
from its office space to its production facilities to ads for the corporate
brand, offers a medium for creating a meaningful transformation. Even
if immediate response appears only superficial, the mere presence of an
ethical commitment can provide an anchor for more substantial changes
at a later time.

In addition, the universal nature of transformative identity establishes
an immediate point of contact with any number of individuals and groups
that do not self-identify with social enterprise. Relieved of the burden of
having to prove that they are special, social entrepreneurs are free to learn
from others who are equally if not identically using their work to create
meaning. This includes the imprudently dismissed nonprofit mainstream,
which more than the movement tends to concede has walked down the
same path. One could go so far as to argue that one of the best ways to
become a successful social entrepreneur is to study something else—there
are, after all, somewhat more technical skills involved in curbing toxic tex-
tile dye emissions or bringing water to the poor than those required to
create a killer pitch deck.

When I began this chapter, I noted that my early experience showed me
how a successful social movement could be marginalized by a lack of due
regard for strategic design. This does not mean, however, that a movement
should set out to be the center of attention. If social enterprise can apply its
core insights to unite what should have never come apart, then its ultimate
success will be to help create a far greater whole.

Chapter 3

HOW CHANGE HAPPENS AND WHY IT SOMETIMES DOESN'T

Ron Schultz
Entrepreneurs4Change

THE DALAI LAMA WALKS UP TO a hot dog vendor and says, "Make me one with everything." The hot dog vendor hands him his hot dog and says, "That will be $2.65." The Dalai Lama gives him three dollars. The vendor puts the money in his pocket and goes back to stirring his onions. The Dalai Lama says, "Excuse me, sir, but what about my change?" The hot dog vendor looks up and says, "Oh, I'm sorry, I thought you knew—change comes from within."

There are tons of clichés about change and its all-pervasive quality, as well as the failure of many things that seem to never change. But contrary to the clichés, there is a very good explanation as to why change happens, and subsequently, why, in many instances, it does not.

If social entrepreneurs are in the business of creating deliberate disruptive design to solve pressing social issues, it is imperative to understand why the changes they seek to bring about succeed and why so many fail.

But perhaps, first, a little history: My own entry into the social entrepreneurial world was neither intentional nor deliberate, but it was certainly disruptive. The fact that my introduction to this world began in my favorite London Pub, the AngleSea, should have prepared me for the way my consciousness was about to be significantly alerted. It didn't.

I was meeting a woman staying in the same B&B as I who had shared over breakfast that she was there to open the European offices for Ashoka: Innovators for the Public. When she described what a social entrepreneur was I knew this was not only what I wanted to do with my life, it would be what I was going to do. I had come to London as a consultant with an expertise in complexity, relationship, and organization, and in a heartbeat, and not a sip of the Guinness before me, I found that the theories of interaction and emergence I had been propounding for years had an application that I had never known existed. And for me it was *the application.*

My work had always been about facilitating change and shifting thinking that was considered intransigent. With the social challenges we faced in our world, I knew I had found what I needed to do. Immediately upon my return to the United States, I began banging on the doors of Ashoka for a job, a pursuit that initially proved to be unsuccessful. Undeterred, I eventually contacted my friend Bob Pratt at Volunteers of America in Los Angeles and told him I thought he should start a social entrepreneurial incubator at VOALA and let me run it, and he agreed. My first call after Bob had said yes, was to Paul Herman (now of HIPInvestor; see chapter six), the fellow at Ashoka who had decided not to hire me. I said simply, "Paul, we have to talk." I was suddenly a social entrepreneur, but I realized I could barely spell it, let alone know what it was I was supposed to do. Paul graciously said, "I think we can work together."

SUCCESS DOESN'T ALWAYS SHOW UP AS EXPECTED

Out of my interaction with this woman from Ashoka, something new and unexpected had emerged for me and had shifted my understanding of the world as I knew it. Recognizing that emergent shift, I also knew I had to do a number of things differently if I wanted that change to really take place. One reason this new understanding was so significant for me was that prior to my arrival in London, I had decided to make a shift in my life to do work that was more significant and truly helped people. But I had no model that made sense to me for doing so until I sat down in that pub and it appeared. Actualizing that model and making the change happen in my life meant a number of things also had to shift. Fortunately, about five years earlier, my colleague and mentor, Howard Sherman, had introduced what was in essence *"a theory of business action"* that described how change takes place. It was amazingly concise and we had written about it in a book we had produced together.[1] It was known as "principles, models, rules, and behaviors."[2]

PRINCIPLES, MODELS, RULES, AND BEHAVIORS

The concept was simple: principles were ideas that because of their nature rarely if ever changed. Models were what we built to emulate principles. Rules were those things we put in place to maintain the model and guide behaviors; and behaviors were what we did to live the principles, based on the models we built and the rules that governed them.

As we unpack this, we can certainly follow my shift in life direction that had originated in London, but I think it would be far more helpful to look at this process in the context of shifting a greater social challenge.

Suppose, for example, we have a principle: "poor people always stay poor." Based on this precept, we then create social models that don't really try and help poor people not be poor, because our principle says they really can't be otherwise. So, instead, we find ways (and models) for applying a salve to ease the issue, but not shift it. The rules we create for supporting organizations that service this issue and that also recognize the principle, however well intended by their design, restrict behaviors because we as a society are unwilling to see this issue differently.

The process fails again and again, and the result is that no real change can ever happen because our principle is flawed. And no matter how diligently we try, nothing new and novel that can effect positive change will ever emerge from our models if the principle is wrong.

But suppose we are capable of making a radical change in our principled position—and we can now say, "Poor people don't have to remain poor." So we hurriedly began reworking the models we've built and come up with a whole new set, because our understanding of how the world works is now completely different. However, in creating these new models, we forget to change the organizational rules that govern them and still support the old principle. The unfortunate result is that behaviors don't change and nothing new happens. But what gets blamed is this—our new principle was obviously wrong, too, because we still got more of the same.

This fight is being borne out in our economic world on a daily basis. The principle that financial corporations would be able to regulate themselves crashed our economy and even though we recognize the principle is wrong and new models and rules are needed, we have refused to implement the changes to the rules, so that in reality no behaviors have changed.

It remains that if we cling to outdated principles—no matter how clever our models—we change nothing. If we change our principles and our models, but still cling to old rules, our behaviors don't change, and we change nothing.

If we change our principles, models, and rules, but keep our old behaviors in place, as had been the case during prohibition, things not only change according to the new design, they can get much worse.

In order for social entrepreneurs to create successful and lasting deliberate disruptive designs, it is imperative to make sure that any new understanding of how the system can work affects not only the principles that govern that understanding—the mission and calling to action that propel many social entrepreneurs—but also the models, rules, and behaviors put in place to turn those ideas into action.

Change can happen, but it only happens when we consciously recognize the fundamental relationship between these four elements and understand the need to adapt them to accommodate our understanding of how our world is currently showing up. But since this book is about practicality—how do we do that? How do we create deliberate disruptive designs that actually make a positive difference in the lives of those for whom they are designed?

A SUSTAINABLE MODEL FOR INCONCEIVABLE DEVELOPMENT

The answer comes in something I call "a sustainable model for inconceivable development,"[3] a methodology and process designed to shift the intransigent. It is both method and practice because it's not something that one does and then is done with it. Once the process is begun, it needs to become an ongoing practice, otherwise, like any living interaction, it will atrophy, stagnate, and ultimately die.

The sustainable model for inconceivable development is a deliberate disruptive design to bring about change. When emergence happens, and we realize that things are not the same as we had previously thought, we are, in essence, changing our understanding of our system and the models we have devised to describe that system. It means that if we really want to realize change, we must adjust our behaviors and relationships according to our new understanding, as well as the rules we have created to maintain that understanding of our system. The sustainable model for inconceivable development starts by:

Step 1: Adjusting our models on the basis of the new understanding that has emerged.

Step 2: Adjusting our relationships, our behavior, and rules according to our new understanding of our model.

Step 3: When we do this something new emerges, because something different always happens whenever there is an interaction between our models and behaviors—once we have taken the first two steps.

Step 4: Returning to step 1—going back and readjusting our models on the basis of this new emergence.

Step 5: Returning to step 2—adjusting our relationships on the basis of our new model.

Step 6: Returning to step 3—emergence happens within the interaction.

Step 7: Returning to step 1—we return to our models, adjusting them according to our new understanding.

Step 8: Returning to step 2—we adjust our relationships again.

Step 9: Returning to step 3—emergence happens.

Step 10: Returning to step 1—the process continues.

This is logical enough and satisfies the intellect, but how does it work in a real-life situation? How, as a social entrepreneur, does this shift the intransigence of the issues I am trying to solve? Let me offer a scenario:

Step 1: I am introduced to a fellow at my favorite coffee shop where I am a regular. He is about 180 degrees opposite from me in political, social, and religious beliefs. If I were to meet him as one of *them*, with all my preconceived notions of who *they* are, nothing changes and the world remains solid. However, if I meet him and I decide to see if we might share some common ground, who knows what might happen. In our initial conversation, I find that even though his beliefs are completely differently from mine, like me, he doesn't like seeing homeless people suffering on the streets. And just like that, here's something we share in common, and my feeling about this person shifts slightly.

Step 2: I begin adjusting my opinion about him and how he shows up in the world.

Step 3: The next day we meet again at the coffee shop and I ask him what he thinks he could do to help a homeless person other than just give them food or money? The response is, "[W]ell, we could give them a job." Suddenly, we're talking about something that relates directly to my world. We sit down with our coffee, and begin talking about what giving "them" a job looks like. I first ask for permission to make a small language change. Instead of the notion of *us* helping *them*, perhaps we can simply refer to this person as a homeless person rather than something other than what we are. When that is accepted, I acknowledge his understanding and say, "You know, I teach entrepreneurship, so, what if it weren't a job, but what would it look like if we helped people in this population start businesses—what would that entail?" The look in his eyes was one that said this was something that had never crossed his mind. As we leave, we shake hands and agree to continue the conversation.

Step 4: As I leave breakfast I'm thinking, "What was that?" My thinking about this person begins to shift again as possibilities start to emerge.

Step 5: The next day over coffee, he has already found a table for us, and the first question about my family is asked and I ask about his. We both have girls. We laugh. The system shifts.

Step: 6: We begin focusing on our ideas from the day before, but there's an enthusiasm about them now that feels different. The conversation turns to what would be required to make this happen. We were both throwing out ideas and both enjoying the exchange. We agree that we would need a curriculum that teaches basic business tenants and teaching it couldn't be rushed. We also agree that we would need mentors to work with each person to help them in areas in which they had no experience. I mention a business professor I know who might be able to convince some of her students to help as mentors.

Step 7: A good part of the rest of my day is spent thinking about this other person who has suddenly taken up my mornings and with whom we seem to be doing, I'm not sure what, but we are doing. The beliefs that are held by us about the world are not important to this or to us doing this together.

Step 8: The next morning we have both invited others to join us. My business professor friend is there as is the head of his church's outreach group, with whom my colleague is friends.

Step 9: A population of homeless people with whom, it turns out, the university and the church have been working is identified. The professor can bring in some students to act as mentors and the church offers its community room to hold classes to begin a joint homeless entrepreneurs' education program. There is great enthusiasm and joy. We all shake hands and laugh struck by what has emerged and the possibilities now before us.

Step 10: The process continues and within four months, the first population of homeless entrepreneurs begins their training. And the process continues.

When adjustments are made after each emergent possibility arises, what we see after the second or third level of emergence is a development that would have been absolutely inconceivable from the perspective of our initial understanding. Our tendency, however, is to stop the process after the first or second level of emergence and close the system back down to protect the initial fabulous innovation that has come about.

The key to sustaining the development process is the continual adjustment of our models, behaviors, and the rules we establish to guide them—our relationships. As soon as we freeze the model, and, subsequently, our relationship to our behaviors, we return to orthodox novelty—the same stuckness with which we began: Conservative and Liberal at loggerheads.

Emergent novelty—real innovation—is possible only when the system is open to what is presently and adjacently possible—those things just one step away from where we are right now. And once the possible becomes present, what was once inconceivable becomes actualized and perhaps Liberals and Conservatives work together.

CHANGE MAY NOT HAPPEN IN OUR LIFETIME—IT'S A PROCESS

The imperative of social entrepreneurs is that we must affect change sooner rather than later and we can't wait for any delays for change to take place. But as Bill Shore, who writes about his process later in this book (see chapter seventeen), wrote in his remarkable book, *The Cathedral Within* (Random House, 1999),[4] those of us engaged in this work must view ourselves as cathedral builders with our labors taking far longer to complete than what might be accomplished in a single lifetime. And, no one person can complete a cathedral alone.

When we fear there isn't time to allow complex interactions and the subsequent emergence to happen, contrary to all logical thinking, we need to stop. We have begun to operate under a principle that is not appropriate to the work that needs to be done, and poor decisions are sure to follow. Our work as social entrepreneurs is to be a conduit to engage others and provide a route over, around, and through the rapids. It is at these times that we also need to address more closely the work unleashed by the previous emergence upon which we are currently acting and the rules we have created to support that model. What has previously emerged fertilizes the ground for the next emergence that will invariably arise, but if we are still holding on to old rules, personal and/or collective, that no longer support what has emerged, there is no room for change and we once again solidify where we are and refuse to do anything differently.

When people are suffering, time feels like the enemy. As social entre-preneurs, however, our job is to audaciously create new channels that can establish whole new flows and directions. As frustrating as it feels, it is not a task that can be accomplished alone or is completed overnight. But change can happen when through our understanding of how the system works, we are willing to shift that understanding and all our relationships to it and then progress forward from that new place.

NOTES

1. Howard Sherman & Ron Schultz, *Open Boundaries: Creating Business Innovation through Complexity* (Perseus Books, 1998).
2 Ron Schultz, "Change, change, change—change of fools," *E:CO* Issue, vol. 14, no. 1 (2012): 95–98.
3. Ron Schultz, "Present Possible, Adjacent Possible, Possibly Possible," *E:CO* Issue, vol. 13, no. 3 (2011): 152–156.
4. Bill Shore, *The Cathedral Within: Transforming Your Life by Giving Something Back* (Random House, 1999).

Chapter 4

LEGAL ISSUES FOR SOCIAL ENTREPRENEURS

Allen R. Bromberger
Perlman and Perlman

UNDERSTANDING THE LEGAL STRUCTURES FACING social entre-preneurs is crucial. These are the rules that govern behavior and influence the models built to shift social disorder. By having a firm grasp of these issues, the legality of our entities can become less of a hindrance and more of the guidepost that they should be. That doesn't imply that these rules can't be changed when they no longer support the new models that have emerged, but to do so, we must know what we are attempting to change, then figure out a way to deliberately disrupt their design.

THE LEGAL STRUCTURES AND THE ENTITIES THEY UPHOLD

Although social enterprises take many forms, from a legal point of view, there are basically five options: a "C" corporation, an "S" corporation, a "nonprofit" corporation, a limited liability company, or a partnership. In addition, there are some special types of entities, such as "benefit" cor-porations and "L3Cs," which are growing in popularity among social entrepreneurs. Another model, the "B" corporation, is not a legal form but rather a certification that is useful primarily for marketing purposes.

"C" corporations are the most common form of business in the United States. Formed primarily to generate profits for their owners, C corporations pay tax on their net income and then pass profits through to the shareholders in the form of dividends, which are taxed as investment income (this is often referred to as the "double tax" on corporate profits). The directors and managers of a C corporation owe their primary allegiance to the shareholders, and have an affirmative duty to maximize profit for the owners. Under traditional jurisprudence, directors of a C corporation are vulnerable to legal challenge if they use the income or assets of the corporation to pursue a social mission at the expense of the shareholders.

"S" corporations are similar to C corporations, except that they don't pay taxes on their net income. Profits are allocated to the shareholders and taxed as ordinary income (usually at a higher rate than investment income). Further, unlike C corporations, which can have multiple classes of shareholders, each with different rights, an S corporation can have only one class of shares, and shareholders must be natural persons; corporations and partnerships cannot own shares in an S corporation.

By contrast, a nonprofit corporation does not issue shares and has no "owners." It is formed for a purpose other than making money (i.e., a social mission), and the directors and managers have an affirmative duty to pursue that social mission for the benefit of the corporations members or the general public. Many nonprofit corporations are tax exempt under section 501(c)(3) of the Internal Revenue Code, which entitles them to receive tax-deductible contributions. However, 501(c)(3) organizations cannot confer benefits on individuals except to the extent they are part of the "charitable class" being served, nor may they pay compensation above a level determined to be "reasonable." They may neither support candidates for public office nor seek to influence legislation to a substantial degree, with some specific exceptions. Finally, the assets and income of a 501(c)(3) organization must be permanently dedicated to charitable purposes, and upon dissolution, any assets must be distributed to other 501(c)(3) organizations formed for similar purposes. 501(c)(3) organizations have to pay a tax on any earned income that is not "substantially related" to its tax-exempt purposes. Income is "related" only if it contributes to the accomplishment of one or more charitable or educational purposes in an important way other than through the production of income. There are 28 other categories of tax exemption that include social welfare organizations, business leagues and chambers of commerce, social and recreational organizations, fraternal societies, title-holding companies, labor unions, Indian tribes, volunteer fire departments, cemetery associations, and nonprofit health care insurance companies. Groups in these categories pay no tax on their net income, but contributions are not tax deductible.

Both C corporations and nonprofit corporations enjoy the benefit of "limited liability." That means that creditors can look only to corporate assets for satisfaction of any liabilities; the shareholders, directors, officers, and employees are not personally liable for corporate obligations.

A limited liability company (LLC) is not a corporation, although it has some similar features, including limited liability. But unlike a corporation, which has a fairly rigid structure and has to live within carefully defined rules and boundaries, an LLC has a more flexible structure and its members can agree among themselves to run the LLC in a manner that suits their own purposes. So, for example, where the directors of a C corporation have to serve the interests of shareholders first, and the directors of a nonprofit corporation have to put social mission first, the members (owners) of an LLC can agree to give profit and social mission equal weight and direct the managers to run the company to accomplish both. Another advantage of the LLC is the fact that an LLC operating agreement can allocate governance rights (decision-making power) and economic rights (a right to profits) in unequal proportions, so that some members (i.e., founders or investors) can have greater economic rights than others, and other members (i.e., founders or managers) can have greater decision-making power than the others.

LLCs have another advantage over C corporations: like S corporations, they do not pay taxes on their net income. Profits are distributed to the owners before tax, albeit as ordinary income. However, LLCs are often preferred over S corporations, because they can have different classes of ownership, each with different rights, and unlike S corporations their shares can be owned by other corporations (nonprofit or for-profit) and even

LLCs, which makes them well-suited for structures that involve subsidiaries and joint ventures.

Partnerships offer the greatest flexibility of all the legal forms. From a legal point of view, partnerships are largely unregulated, and partners can agree among themselves to almost any structure or arrangement. However unlike corporations and LLCs, partnerships do not have "limited liability": the partners are personally liable for the obligations of the partnerships, which puts their personal assets at risk. The exception to this is for "limited partnerships," in which one partner—the general partner—operates the partnership and is entirely at risk, and the other partners—the limited partners—play the role of passive investors and only their investments are at risk.

Like C corporations, S corporations, LLCs, and partnerships can accept investment in the form of equity or debt. Nonprofit corporations cannot issue equity, but they can incur debt.

JURISDICTIONAL CONSIDERATIONS

Corporations, LLCs, and partnerships are creatures of state law, and the laws that govern them, while substantially similar in all jurisdictions, can vary in important respects from state to state. So, for example, the rights of minority shareholders may receive greater protection in one state than another. Or the rules for approving corporate actions may require a shareholder vote in one state but not in another. But most people are blissfully unaware of these distinctions. Founders typically set up companies either in the state where they will be operating, or in Delaware, which has very lenient laws and relatively little regulation, and is therefore the jurisdiction of choice for many new companies.

For social entrepreneurs, the most important factor when choosing a state in which to form the company is the degree to which the directors and managers of the company are permitted to take social mission into consideration when making business decisions. Delaware, for example, is hostile to this notion, and case law in Delaware forces corporate directors to place the short-term economic interests of the shareholders above all other considerations. So if you have a Delaware company, and you want to sell the company to a buyer who will pay a fair price and keep the social mission, as opposed to a buyer who will pay a higher price and eliminate the social mission, you can't do it. You have to take the highest bid. That's true even if the majority of the shareholders want to take the lower bid. Other states, especially the 30 states that have adopted so-called constituency statutes, take a different position. The law in those states expressly permits corporate directors to take a broad range of factors—including the impact on the environment and employees—into consideration when making business decisions.

Some states have even gone further, recognizing special kinds of corporations and LLCs that are specifically designed for social enterprise. The strongest of these is the "benefit" corporation. It is similar to a normal C corporation, but the directors are required (not just permitted) to take the interests of the community, the environment, and the interests of stakeholders (customers, employees, and suppliers) into account when making business decisions. In exchange, the directors are given strong protection against legal liability. Another form, the "L3C," is similar to a normal LLC, but it has to be formed specifically to further charitable and educational goals, and profit has to take a backseat to the accomplishment of those goals.

RAISING CAPITAL: THE OFFERING PROCESS

In the life of almost every successful social enterprise, there comes a point when the owners of the business must ask whether they should raise additional capital by seeking outside investors. That's not news. But what most social entrepreneurs *don't* know is that any time a business entity approaches third parties seeking investment in an enterprise, state and federal securities laws come into play.

The most important of these laws is the Federal Securities Act of 1933. That law requires companies to give investors (and potential investors) full disclosure of all "material facts"—facts that investors would find important in making an investment decision—whenever they offer any kind of security to the public.

A "security" is broadly defined to include (1) stocks, bonds, notes, puts, calls, options, certificates of deposit, or a group or index of securities or derivatives thereof (in general, any interest or instrument commonly known as a "security"), and (2) any warrant or right to subscribe to or purchase any of the foregoing. In other words, just about any kind of investment or loan you can imagine, however structured, is covered by the law.

PUBLIC OFFERINGS

Under the Securities Act of 1933, any offering of securities *to the general public* has to be registered with the SEC before the security can be offered for sale. Registration allows the SEC to review the terms of the investment and the offering to make sure that they provide full disclosure of the information a potential investor should have in order to make an informed investment decision. The process of registering a public offering is expensive and time consuming, and as a practical matter, it is simply not an option for most social enterprises.

Fortunately, the law provides four situations in which an enterprise may solicit investors without having to file an offering with the SEC:

1. You may "test the waters," using general solicitation and advertising prior to filing an offering statement with the SEC. This gives you the advantage of determining whether there is enough market interest in your securities before you incur the full range of legal, accounting, and other costs associated with filing an offering statement. You may not, however, solicit or accept money until the SEC staff completes its review of the filed offering statement and you deliver prescribed offering materials to investors.
2. You may make an "intrastate offering"; that is, you may offer the security for sale in one state only to residents of that state without filing with the SEC (but you may have to register with state authorities).
3. You may make a "friends and family" offering, by limiting your solicitation only to family members and close personal friends (unfortunately, "friends of friends" don't qualify).
4. Finally, you can do a "private placement" by limiting the solicitation to "accredited investors" plus a limited number of other persons.

For most social enterprises, the private placement is the strategy of choice. The key to a private placement is that it is offered only to a limited number of investors, and if the investors are "accredited" (see later), the disclosure requirements are flexible. A "private placement memorandum" or "PPM" is often used to make the offering. A PPM is a legal document, which provides full disclosure to potential investors. It is typically accompanied by subscription agreements or loan and participation agreements, which investors use (a) to indicate their desire to make the investment and (b) certify the fact that they are qualified to buy the security (i.e., they are an accredited investor.)

The preparation of a PPM is normally done with the assistance of a qualified attorney and should only be done by someone with substantial experience in business planning and a deep familiarity with the enterprise itself. While there is no specific form for the PPM, it does have to follow certain technical requirements, and it must include various disclosures and disclaimers required under federal and state law.

Private placements are governed by Regulation D of the Securities Act of 1933. There are three kinds of private placements under Regulation D, each of which allows a company to raise different amounts of money from different kinds of investors (i.e., accredited and nonaccredited), and each imposes different resale and transfer restrictions on the investors.

Under the securities law, an accredited investor includes any of the following:

- a bank, insurance company, registered investment company, business development company, or small business investment company;
- an employee benefit plan, within the meaning of the Employee Retirement Income Security Act, if a bank, insurance company, or registered investment adviser makes the investment decisions, or if the plan has total assets in excess of $5 million;
- a charitable organization, corporation, or partnership with assets exceeding $5 million;
- a director, executive officer, or general partner of the company selling the securities;
- a business in which all the equity owners are accredited investors;
- a natural person who has individual net worth, or joint net worth with the person's spouse, that exceeds $1 million at the time of the purchase;

- a natural person with income exceeding $200,000 in each of the two most recent years or joint income with a spouse exceeding $300,000 for those years and a reasonable expectation of the same income level in the current year; or
- a trust, including a charitable trust, with assets in excess of $5 million, not formed to acquire the securities offered, whose purchases are made by a sophisticated person.

The private placement offering process itself is also regulated and follows certain norms. Typically, the process begins with the creation of a business plan, including projections of how much needs to be raised and who the likely investors will be. The business plan is used to create the PPM and the subscription or loan participation agreement. New investors subscribe to purchase the securities being offered by returning a signed subscription or loan participation agreement to the company. The directors of the company then vote whether or not to accept each investor; once an investor is approved and the cash or services used to pay for the securities is tendered to the company, a purchase or loan agreement is signed and the security is issued to the investor. The company then has to file a form with the SEC disclosing that the sale has occurred. If you are dealing with a group of new investors, it helps to arrange things so that you can do the approvals (and the SEC filing) for all the new investors as a group.

If the offering company is an LLC, the process is the same, except that the subscription has to be approved by the members of the LLC and the operating agreement usually has to be amended. This can vary from case to case depending on the law of the state where the LLC is formed, or based on provisions in the operating agreement itself.

If the offering discloses proprietary information, trade secrets, or other sensitive material, it is standard practice to have anyone who receives a copy of the PPM to sign a "nondisclosure agreement" (NDA) before they receive the PPM, just to be safe. In some cases, the nondisclosure agreement is actually integrated into the PPM itself. The nondisclosure agreement prevents the recipient of the information from disclosing it to anyone else. Here, too, you need a lawyer who knows what he or she is doing. You can "borrow" someone else's agreement, but if it contains provisions that don't apply to you, or is flawed in some other way, it may not be enforceable.

In addition to the federal compliance requirements outlined earlier, you may also need to register with one or more states as a "broker-dealer" or an "issuer-dealer." Many states require anyone who is soliciting investments within the state to notify the state (usually the attorney general's office) that they are doing so. This usually involves filing additional form(s) and the payment of filing fee(s) in any state where an offeree resides. In order to properly advise you about this, you will need to discuss where your potential investors are located with your attorney, so that he or she can determine what each state requires in this regard.

EQUITY COMPENSATION

Equity compensation occurs when someone is given stock (or the option to buy stock) in a company in exchange for services. Typically, equity compensation is used to provide incentives for employees to join a company or work for less money in exchange for a chance to participate in the profits of the company if it is successful. Since the value of the stock (or option) can be very high if the company is successful, and it may be worthless if the company is not, equity compensation serves to align the interests of employees and investors, and it also allows the company to recruit and retain talent using its stock as a form of currency.

Equity compensation can take several forms. One way is by a direct grant of stock (or the option to buy stock at a predefined price) to an individual employee or a group of individual employees. Stock options are sometimes preferred by employers because the employee does not actually own stock until the option is exercised. However, recent changes in the tax treatment of stock options has reduced their attractiveness to employees, so they may not be as effective in attracting and retaining talent as direct grants of stock. Stock options typically take one of two forms: an incentive stock option (ISO) may be granted to employees only, and the exercise price of the ISO must be equal to or greater than the stock's fair market value on the grant date. A nonqualified stock option (NQSO) may be granted to nonemployees, such as outside directors or advisors. The exercise price of NQSOs may also be less than the stock's fair market value on the grant date. Both ISOs and NQSOs are regulated by federal tax law, and the tax and accounting implications, which are beyond the scope of this chapter, have to be carefully considered before a decision to offer them is made.

Typically, grants of stock or options are subject to restrictions, the most common of which is the requirement that they "vest" through the passage of time or the happening of an event. Such awards are also typically subject to restrictions on transfer or exercise, to prevent the employee from selling them or acquiring the rights in a way that defeats the purpose of giving the grant in the first place. So, for example, if you have a chief technology officer to whom you've granted the right to buy stock as a way to keep him or her working for you, you may restrict his or her ability to sell the stock for three years, and provide that if he or she leaves the company before then, the stock (or option) is forfeit.

Another way to give employees an ownership interest in a company is by creating an "employee stock ownership plan" (ESOP). An ESOP is a plan that grants all employees of a company an interest in the company, typically based on their length of service, as a way to reward loyalty and recognize the employee's collective contributions to the company's success. ESOPs are governed by federal pension laws, specifically the Employee Retirement Income Security Act (ERISA). ERISA sets forth clear requirements to ensure that there can be no "preferred" classes of participants in an ESOP; all employees must be treated proportionally the same.

PROTECTING YOUR INTELLECTUAL PROPERTY

NONDISCLOSURE AGREEMENTS

As noted earlier, an NDA is a document that requires the recipient of proprietary information to keep it confidential. To be binding, it has to be signed by the recipient. In discussing business ideas, potential products or services, marketing campaigns, or even business plans with potential investors, it is always good to have an NDA. As a practical matter, however, many potential partners or investors may refuse to sign NDAs as a matter of policy, out of fear that the NDA may prevent them from pursuing a similar business opportunity with someone else if they don't make a deal with you. In these cases, the entrepreneur has to weigh the risk of someone stealing his or her ideas against the risk that they may not be able to negotiate a deal that could be beneficial or even essential to the success of their company.

TRADEMARK, COPYRIGHT, AND PATENT

Trademarks protect names and logos (or anything that uniquely identifies the supplier of goods or services) from anyone that wants to use a confusingly similar mark to identify themselves as the provider of similar goods or services. The purpose of the trademark is to protect consumers—by making sure they know who they are dealing with when they buy goods or services in the marketplace. Trademarks are also the most potent way to protect a brand.

Trademarks are established by actual use in commerce—if you don't use a mark to actually identify goods and services to the market, you don't get any protection. Additional and important protection comes from registering trademarks, typically with the US Patent and Trademark Office (USPTO), although you can also register marks at the state level. Registration is straightforward—you provide a copy of the mark to the USPTO, identify the class of goods or services for which you are using it (i.e., consulting services or manufacturing), and pay a fee. If the USPTO decides the mark is not too similar to an already existing mark, and it is unique enough (i.e., it isn't merely generic or descriptive), they will register it. That puts the world on notice that you are using the mark and provides protection against anyone who later comes along and tries to use a mark that is confusingly similar to yours.

Copyright, by contrast, grants "authors" a bundle of exclusive rights with respect to their work. These rights include the right to reproduce, distribute, perform, publicly display, or create derivative works based on the original work. Under the copyright law, the creator of the original expression in a work is its author. While use of a copyright notice, for example, ©2012 John Doe, was once required as a condition of copyright protection, it is now optional; the author is protected even if no copyright notice is placed on the work. The author is automatically considered to be the owner of copyright unless there is a written agreement by which the author assigns the copyright to another person or entity, such as a publisher or an employer. Many employment policies and contracts contain "work for hire" provisions, which makes the employer or the commissioning party the author for copyright purposes. Work for hire provisions are generally enforceable. Copyright protection can also be lost if the work is placed in the public domain.

A patent is a right granted by the government of the United States of America to an inventor "to exclude others from making, using, offering for sale, or selling the invention throughout the United States or import-ing the invention into the United States" for a limited time in exchange for public disclosure of the invention when the patent is granted. Patents are an extremely powerful form of protection: If you have a patent, you can prevent anyone else from using the invention that is covered by the patent, *even if they discovered it themselves independently.* There are three types of patents. *Utility patents* may be granted to anyone who invents or discovers any new and useful process, machine, article of manufacture, or composi-tion of matter, or any new and useful improvement thereof. *Design patents* may be granted to anyone who invents a new, original, and ornamental design for an article of manufacture. *Plant patents* may be granted to any-one who invents or discovers and asexually reproduces any distinct and new variety of plant. The process of obtaining a patent is complicated and technical, and you can lose patent protection easily by not following the rules. For example, if you disclose your invention to others without the protection of an NDA, and you don't file a patent application within strict time limits, you lose your ability to patent the invention. If you think you may have a patentable invention, you should consult with a patent attorney as soon as possible.

LICENSING IP

The owner of a trademark, copyright, patent, or other intellectual property can allow others to use the protected property by granting them a license to do so. Intellectual property licenses take many different forms, but typi-cally they consist of a contract or agreement by which the owner of the property grants to someone else the right to use it, subject to appropriate restrictions, in exchange for a royalty. In addition to private agreements, some owners of intellectual property can grant rights to the general public to use the work within certain limits, such as the obligation to attribute the work. One popular source of these kinds of license are the "creative commons" licenses that have been developed by experts to facilitate the process of allowing the public to use protected works without placing them in the public domain, which could destroy the owner's rights. Anther closely related form of license is the "open source" license.

EXITS

In the life of social enterprises, there are times when the founder or the investors decide that they want to exchange some or all of their ownership in the company for cash or something else of value. These are commonly referred to as "exit" events. They can take several forms.

The simplest and cleanest way to exit ownership of a company is to sell the company, or at least the shares, membership certificates, or other security that represents the seller's ownership interest. If the entire company is to be sold, this involves selling all the shares. In these transactions, the shareholders have to approve the transaction, and dissenting minority shareholders are entitled to some protections. However, if someone buys the entire company, they are not only buying the company's assets, but its liabilities as well. Cautious buyers will want to avoid this, as it can be hard to determine what liabilities might be lurking out there. Instead, many buyers prefer to buy the company's assets directly, and an "asset sale" is often the preferred form of transaction.

In an asset sale, the assets to be purchased are typically identified and appraised in order to determine the price. As with a sale of the company, sale of all or a substantial portion of a company's assets requires the consent of the shareholders, and the managers and directors of the company have an obligation to disclose all the material terms of the transaction as part of that process. Once the assets are sold, it is normal (but not required) for the shareholders to pay off all obligations and liabilities of the company and then dissolve it. This involves additional time and expense. But once dissolved, the company is "gone," and no one remains responsible for anything.

Another option for exit is to merge or consolidate two or more companies into one. In a merger, the assets and liabilities of both companies are combined, and the ownership interests are restructured according to the terms of the merger. For example, in a merger, it is possible for the shareholders of one company to end up with a larger or smaller share of the combined company. However, the larger company may be stronger and more attractive to a buy-out by new or existing investors. Or the terms of the merger itself may provide for some of the shareholders to receive cash or other consideration in exchange for their shares.

One final option for exit is to dissolve the company. A dissolution essentially shuts down the company. This may be preceded (not necessarily) by a sale of assets. In some cases, when a company is not successful, and the owners do not want to invest any more capital, they may choose to shut the company down rather than continue it as a going concern. Going through the legal process of dissolution winds down the company and ends its legal existence in a clean, safe, orderly manner.

While much of this may seem technical and something that should be shunted off to someone else to deal with, as a social entrepreneur, it is imperative that you understand what you are getting into. Ignorance of the law just means you're ignorant. It doesn't protect you. Take the time to know and understand the rules that govern your behavior. If you don't like them, change them, but don't just ignore them. Following that approach is liable to find you in jail or at least in court. And while there are those who have affected great change from the confines of a jail cell, or by court victory over matters of principle, they are usually there by choice, not there because of their own ignorance.

Chapter 5

SOCIAL MARKETING: INFLUENCING BEHAVIOR FOR SOCIAL IMPACT

Alan R. Andreasen
McDonough School of Business,
Georgetown University

SOCIAL ENTERPRISES ARE CREATIVE APPROACHES to bringing about important—and some not-so-important—changes in the lives of individuals and of the societies of which they are a part. They can be carried out by corporations, nongovernmental organizations, and, in some countries, government agencies. To succeed, they need to find ways to get a wide range of individuals to take actions. Central, of course, are behaviors vital to the social enterprise's mission—getting people to take up a recommended action such as not smoking, starting a business, allowing their daughters to get advanced schooling, washing their hands regularly, installing energy-saving appliances in their homes, and so forth. But the social enterprise has a great many other constituencies to take actions—governments to give contracts or give permission for a particular initiative, volunteers to help out, corporations to partner, foundations or philanthropists to give grants, and individuals to volunteer as advisors or board members. And finally, because they are social enterprises, they are expected to generate sales for their artist works, food services, or used clothing!

Behavior is key. And that is what *marketing* is all about. In the private sector, it is about getting you and me to buy a product, use our service, go to our website, subscribe to our magazine or our weight loss program. And marketers are very good at this. It is an appreciation of this simple fact that gave rise to the field of social marketing—the application of concepts and tools from the private sector to bring about the kinds of behaviors described earlier—behaviors that do not yield profits (except as a means not an end) but make individuals' lives better and/or improve the society of which they are a part.

Social marketing has a surprisingly long history but it is only in the last 20 years that it has come into its own. And, with the burgeoning interest in social enterprise, it is poised to have an even wider impact.

SOME HISTORY

Social marketing had its origins in the early days of family planning in India. In most of the developing world in the 1960s and 1970s, economic development expenditures were growing commerce but people were becoming worse off because families were producing children faster than the economy was growing! Some business school professors visiting in India looked at the traditional free public sector approach and thought that there had to be a better way—and the better way was using commercial marketing concepts and tools to fundamentally reduce the rate of population growth. This meant branding condoms and pills (often the same products as available in government clinics), advertising widely and imaginatively, and insuring that the distribution of products was both widespread and *reliable*. These simple principles soon applied in more and more countries have had an amazing impact—as readers of this volume are well aware.

Social entrepreneurs seeking change in an increasingly wide range of social problems took heed. Organizations applied social marketing concepts and tools to a range of child survival problems—measles, diarrhea, upper respiratory infections, iodine deficiencies—and soon the scourge of HIV/AIDS. At the same time, the academic community and marketing professors saw the social marketing concept as opening up a whole new area of research and teaching. Led by marketing guru Philip Kotler and his colleagues at Northwestern business school, academic studies began to appear, textbooks were written, and lectures given under the rubric of "the broadened marketing concept."

The field grew slowly with the vast majority of applications in health and with an emphasis on the advertising/promotion dimension of social marketing campaigns. Two developments in the 1990s and 2000s significantly both tightened and broadened the field's purview. On the one hand, both practitioners and scholars agreed that the "bottom line" of social marketing is *behavior*—not intentions, not knowledge, not agreement with some ideas. This, it was pointed out, is central to private sector marketing—one is not rewarded for having people love your brand if it does not lead to sales! On the other hand, social marketers began to pay much more attention to the fact that for individuals to act, there are very often key individuals in their environment that have to act. If a child is obese, parents, school principals, and food marketers have to act so that the child can both reduce caloric intake and exercise more (e.g., on a scary school ground).

And, today, the field has a new image problem—making clear that social media marketing is *not* what is meant by social marketing. And, in my own case, I have begun to argue—as in the introduction—that in the world of social enterprise, many other individuals need to act if one is to be successful; these include staff, board members, partners, volunteers, funders, and government officials. It is all about behavior and social marketers have frameworks that potentially can apply to all these situations.

CONCEPTS AND TOOLS

If one's goal is to get someone to act, it is critical to have a well thought out, consistent approach to all such situations. Over the years, others and I have come to rely on some basic approaches. Let me suggest four that I have found useful.

First is MOA. If we expect someone to act, they need to be "motivated." But, as private sector marketers are well aware, if they do not have the "opportunity" (a nearby store or easily accessible website), they can't act. And, if they do not have the "ability" to act (credit options or some advice on how to use the product), then also they can't act. Similarly, for our obese child to act, he or she needs *motivation* but also *opportunity* in the form of healthy cafeteria offerings and safe playgrounds and *ability* in his or her understanding of what constitutes healthy eating and how much exercise of what type is needed.

The second concept is sometimes called "stages of change." The notion is straightforward but is often not how social entrepreneurs approach behavioral challenges. That is, the latter tend to see the behavior challenge as getting someone not doing something desirable to do it. But our own experience tells us, new behaviors—especially challenging ones—take time. The "stages" idea is really a segmentation approach suggesting that some target audiences will be in "precontemplation"—they may not know they need to act or think that acting doesn't apply to them ("my family has all been heavy"). The challenge here is not action but getting them to stage 2—"contemplation" or thinking about possibly taking steps. Then there is "preparation and action"—some people may not act because of ability and opportunity barriers that need to be attended to. And if they act and if the behavior is one they need to continue—keep exercising, stay off drugs—then attention to the "maintenance" stage will be important for this group.

The next concept is most important and is related to the first two. That is, to induce someone to act, one really needs insight into what they are thinking. As P&G and Ford marketers will tell you, great marketers are ones who listen deeply to their customers. They see their challenge is to take customers as they find them and create strategies that respond to what they have heard. Too many social innovators in my experience start with the wrong mindset—seeing the target audience as the problem and setting themselves the challenge of straightening them out.

I have found a simple acronym—BCOS—helpful in guiding my research and thinking about studying and influencing target audiences. It is based on several social scientists—but social entrepreneurs don't want "science," they want everyday approaches they can carry around mentally and apply whenever they have somebody they want to influence, be it someone with a social problem or a boss who isn't being helpful!. The four elements of BCOS are:

Benefits: It is important to understand what the target audience sees— or might see—as the benefits of the action you are advocating. They might see some things you do not and they may be missing some points that you feel may sway their thinking.

Costs: Unfortunately too many social marketers take audience reluctance as a reason to hammer away at the benefits again and again. But commercial marketers know that if a product is seen as hard to use, maybe the answer is trying to motivate and teach the customer to try harder—but change the product! So, in social marketing, it is crucial to understand what the target audience thinks are the costs of doing what you want. In my own experience, the costs may well be not at all what you think. And, you need to minimize them if not get them totally out of the way.

Others: People often do not act—no matter what they think—because others don't want them to. This is a significant problem in the developing world where "western" innovations in health or schooling or commerce are introduced. And, of course, social influence can be a very positive force behind your desired action—as the Internet has proven (even in the developing world).

Self-efficacy: This awkwardly labeled term simply highlights the O and A factors noted earlier in the chapter. Does the target audience feel that they have the opportunity and ability to act—not whether you think they do!

The final concept is one that is constantly in the mind of every private-sector marketer—competition. Target audiences have much going on in their lives that may take priority over what you want. Competitors may be urging other actions or no behavior at all. It is important to see what target audiences perceive as competition and, if so, one needs to understand what they offer and how you can make the case that your option is superior!

DOES IT WORK?

By now, the field of social marketing is replete with a range of effective applications and a number of advances in frameworks not unlike those outlined in this chapter. There are now journals and textbooks, readers and handbooks, and a number of websites and centers with tools and examples. Conferences occur regularly and academics and practitioners alike are slowly advancing the evidence base and underlying explanatory models to increase the scientific underpinnings of the field even farther.

One example that illustrates the approach and its potential impact is an old but a powerful one. The challenge was—and still is—teenage smoking. In the 1990s, despite years of public service announcements and government actions in the United States and in many developed countries, smokers—especially teens—were not responding to conventional approaches. Fortunately, two things happened toward the end of the decade. First, after years of court battles, the tobacco industry finally caved in to mounting legal pressure—not from individuals but from states' attorneys general. The major manufacturers agreed to change many of their practices and pay out substantial settlement amounts to states, amounts that would continue for years! And in the course of litigation, a wealth of documentation surfaced about what the leading tobacco marketers were doing to attract teen smokers, who were essential to the industry's continued sales and profits.

Second, a new approach based on social marketing concepts and tools was created and implemented to great effect in Florida. The state was one of the first to get tobacco settlement money and Governor Lawton Childs made sure that a significant portion of the money would go into programs to reduce teen smoking. Initial research surfaced two key findings. First, teens saw past antismoking advertising as an effort by adults to get them to change, threatening them with major long-term health effects. Teens knew the latter and resented the former. Second, when asked why they smoked, a common motivation they admitted to was "rebellion!" As a result of these key insights, the Florida Tobacco Pilot Program developed an approach that (a) involved teens talking to teens and (b) offered teens rebellion if they quit or resisted taking smoking up. The rebellion they offered was against the tobacco industry that was trying to influence (control?) them to becoming smokers.

The campaign, called the "Truth Campaign," was immensely successful and was subsequently adopted and implemented nationwide by the American Legacy Foundation, which was created to manage the vast sums disgorged from the master settlement agreement that covered all US states and territories.

The main points to emphasize are that this was a campaign started with research listening to teen targets so that the campaign understood in depth what was going on in the heads of the individuals they were trying to influence. Then, the creative staff found ways to promise benefits that members of the target audience said were important. They brought social pressure to bear from other teens and helped develop quit-smoking programs to deal with self-efficacy issues for teens that needed help creating and maintaining a tobacco-free lifestyle. Declines in teen smoking rates in Florida were dramatic and proved equally so when the approach rolled out nationally.

Social marketers have learned that a target audience focus is essential to behavioral influence whether in the private sector or in the public domain. Social entrepreneurs benefit significantly by recognizing that a social marketing "mindset" and approach can be a powerful methodology for them in a wide range of situations and programs where others need to act—and keep on acting—if social change is to happen. Social marketers are constantly gaining—and sharing—new insights and new frameworks about how to get things done. The twenty-first century will see even more impressive developments as social enterprise becomes even more pervasive and impactful in changing people's lives around the world.

Chapter 6

MEASURING THE IMPACT OF SOCIAL ENTREPRENEURSHIP

R. Paul Herman
HIP Investor Inc.

THEORY AND GENESIS OF HIP

Do good. Make money. Most people today consider only one path—do good or make money. Many people presume a tradeoff—the more good, the less money you can make. The more money, the less good you can foster. All of this presumes tradeoffs, rather than innovative approaches that can do both.

Do good *and* make money. Now, there's a theme to rally around. Most new graduates building a career today presume there's no other path than to do both at the same time. A generation of social entrepreneurs has also broken the "good + profit" barrier with financially sustainable nonprofits such as Kiva.org, and high positive impact enterprises such as Compartamos. com, a publicly listed microfinance and banking institution in Mexico.

Yet in our brains, bones, and soul, we feel this combination of "good + profit" is possible in all industries, in all sectors, across all of society. Yet an industry full of innovation remains one of the laggards in this new way of thinking: the financial services sector.

From banks to investment advisors to brokers to venture capitalists, most of the "experts" in these fields still refuse to open their eyes to a world where positive "human impact" and potential profit are possible at the same time. These financial professionals, who are supposed to arbitrage every opportunity ignored by the market, are losing out on money-making opportunities—their raison d'être, or reason for being.

The vision for HIP started when I was at Ashoka.org, which finds, funds, and accelerates social entrepreneurs globally. After a business entrepreneur (the typical donor to Ashoka) requested ways that 95 percent of their portfolio could generate positive impact, just like their 5 percent donation to Ashoka, I researched several microfinance deals that could meet that "impact + profit" goal. However, while the entrepreneur was enthusiastic, he required his advisor to approve anything new. Despite microfinance being lower risk and potentially higher returns than traditional banking, the financial advisor rejected this opportunity.

Was it lower risk? Yes, the financial advisor admitted. Did it offer higher-return potential? Again, "yes" was the advisor's answer. Well then, why wasn't this a portfolio fit? Because it was "social" and "would never work" said the advisor. But microfinance had a multiyear track record of social and financial successes by that point. No matter to the advisor, they had made up their mind.

In fact, there are a multitude of opportunities to generate impact and profit at the same time. A simple way to view this is to quantify the human, social, and environmental impact on one axis of a 2×2 grid (a favorite of former management consultants; I am an alumnus of McKinsey), while plotting the profit margin on the second axis of that grid. When investments of all types are analyzed, there are examples in each quadrant (see figure 6.1): high impact and high profit is one of them.

This insight—that humans can create both impact and profit—is the foundation of our work at HIP Investor. "HIP" stands for "human impact + profit." We see a world where entrepreneurs create value for society by solving everyday human problems, and designing a business approach that generates revenues, employs people, and can be profitable. Examples today range from organic milk (where demand continues to outstrip supply), renewable energy (some of which has zero variable cost for years, like wind

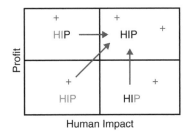

Figure 6.1 Investment analysis: high impact and high profit

or sun), and tools for better learning (like language classes, which expand employment potential as well as create multicultural opportunities).

The HIP Scorecard is a tool to quantify, rate, and rank all types of organizations, ventures, and corporations—and all varieties of investment opportunities. Investors of capital—whether it be equity, debt, or even grants—should expect to evaluate all investments on three criteria: risk, return, and impact. In fact, focusing on human, social, and environmental impact has the potential to reduce risk and enhance returns. Again, the financial industry has ignored this for several decades—which has led to more volatility, less investment in new opportunities, and a system that is preventing new models from innovating and emerging to build a better world in the twenty-first century.

APPLICATION OF HIP

Having so-called financial experts who treasure data to fund new ideas, reject a new investment opportunity out of emotional bias, ignorance, and lack of possibility was frustrating to me—and did push my buttons to action. With an analytical father, curious mother, and analytical training from Wharton and McKinsey, I was compelled to collect the data, analyze the true performance, and if necessary invest in the portfolios that showcased this potential "human impact + profit."

With the enthusiasm of an army of interns trained to find, understand, and interpret impact of the largest one hundred companies by market value, we set out to quantify the "intangible" values and link them to the financial statements. Setting up a spectrum of impact metrics is not easy, but it's doable—just like science: sometimes hard, but solvable. One simplifying approach was that the core human needs (which Dr. Abraham Maslow's hierarchy outlines) were five excellent categories of what all humans seek: health, wealth, earth, equality, and trust.

These five categories allowed metrics to be grouped in each segment. They also enabled entrepreneurs to select which human issues they wanted to address through products and services they sold, as well as organize a supply chain. Investors too can choose which of those five—or a combination of all of them—matched their investment goals. This simplifying approach enabled a summary score to be calculated for impact, from one to one hundred.

All types of organizations and ventures can be rated on their absolute and relative impact—by the factors of health, wealth, earth, equality, and trust. This creates the conditions for a marketplace to match organizations, entrepreneurs, and investors all seeking a similar outcome—a better world expressed by quantified realizations of impact. HIP has calculated scores for more than three thousand companies globally, incorporating metrics ranging across customer satisfaction, employee engagement, fossil-fuel efficiency, talent diversity, and transparency of reporting.

What results is a constructive "race to the top" among firms. As each organization has people (even Exxon and Halliburton), many employees don't want to be ranked low or last—especially if the criteria are how you help other humans, the environment, or society. Thus, by rating impact across all types of organizations, a HIP Scorecard spurs this competition defined as the core that quantifies "doing more good" as well as the detailed financials focused on "making more money."

With this HIP approach, we can plot the impact scores and the profit margins (positive or negative) on a 2×2 grid (like we described earlier) and start to see who are leaders in "doing good" while also "making money." Entrepreneurs can then compete for capital and talent by demonstrating their leadership in both dimensions—impact and profit—and investors can allocate capital and expertise more appropriately as well.

HIP IN PRACTICE

One family office, Meyer Family Enterprises, has chosen to embed this entire approach into all of their investing of capital and expertise. Bonny

Meyer and Patrick Gleeson have written an investment policy statement that requires the portfolio to seek the goal of "100% invested for impact by 2020," the end of the decade. That's like President John F. Kennedy declaring the "moonshot," safe landing and return to Earth, in the early 1960s.

To achieve that vision, MFE has adapted the HIP Scorecard into a simplified version called the "HIP Check," with additional questions like "do you want to have a beer with the entrepreneur?" and "how many of the staff work more than 40 hours per week?" in addition to "how diverse is your team, executives, and board?" and "what is your estimated carbon footprint?" These questions focus on long-term human sustainability as well as the likelihood of collaboration among investors and entrepreneurial leaders. MFE uses the HIP Check for evaluating new investments as well as teeing up divestments from the portfolio.

Measuring the progress toward that visionary 2020 goal of 100 percent invested for impact requires a regular report card on each investment in the portfolio. These investments have different profiles of the three core investor criteria: risk, return, and impact. In each investment report, MFE reviews an overall picture of how much good, and how much risk-adjusted return—across every investment type (from venture capital and private equity, to real estate and hedge funds, to public equity and debt, to municipal bonds and cash).

This approach seems like a radical path for most investors and their financial advisors. They question these new fundamentals, which can be leading indicators of business success and potentially stronger portfolios. They are skeptical that self-interest and group-interest can overlap in a capitalist economy. The focus on historical track record is so embedded that it represses any new innovation.

Meanwhile, on the company side, we get calls from the "most HIP" of our rated companies, which recognize the communication of sustainability performance to the general public. Public relations firms call HIP quarterly wanting to know the latest results of our HIP Scorecard—and whether their position has increased or decreased, and which competitors they are beating or lagging. This competitive nature is built into our human DNA—and our daily life.

However, because "quality of life," "well-being," and "human impact" don't easily compute into a score, most people and the financial industry focus on the amounts in trading accounts, bank balances, and retirement plans. What is missed, which impact investors already see, is that profit is only gained when you solve a human need first. Health, wealth, earth, equality, and trust are categories of impact that we all want and need. Thus, by building a business or organization around serving those needs, and counting the positive and negative factors numerically in impact metrics, we can more confidently migrate to a life that is fuller, a society that is more supportive of each of our goals and dreams, and an economy that is self-sustaining financially as well as preserving our planet's natural resources.

My entire life has focused on blending the power of metrics from all disciplines into a system that harmonizes self-interest and group-interest. Whether developing a scorecard for energy utilities or public utility commissions early in my career, or building a financial services platform for kids, teens, and parents to manage money together, or helping investors seek the highest levels of human impact and potential profit—it is clear that we the people are simultaneously competitive and collaborative. Just like sports, we like to team up, and battle to win together (or lose while trying).

The HIP Scorecard approach brings together everything I have learned in my life to date—that the invisible values of life, previously unmeasured by experts, can be quantified into a metric; this summary score can translate into a competitive position and drive human action toward a common goal: a more fulfilling society that supports our joint quest for human potential. That potential can be captured in five elements: health, wealth, earth, equality, and trust. And if we can harness the power of capitalism, which mobilizes land, labor, and capital faster than any other system toward a goal of "human impact + profit," that is a world in which each of us individually, and collectively as a society, would produce feelings of happiness, and fulfillment of our own dreams for a life of purpose and achievement.

Chapter 7

EVALUATING COMPLEX CHANGE

Glenda H. Eoyang
Human Dynamic Systems Institute

AS A SOCIAL ENTREPRENEUR YOU ARE CONSTANTLY undergoing a variety of evaluations. Funders monitor your work and ask you to report on your performance. You monitor and provide feedback to employees, subcontractors, volunteers, and partners. Evaluation results focus and motivate continuing investment of individual and collective energy. Even when your vision of the future is clear and persistent, you need feedback from your complex environment to adjust and adapt strategy as circumstances change and as you move closer to your goal. Besides all this, successful leaders produce results, so you only know your success when you see evidence of your results.

On the other hand, evaluation should not be a "one size fits all" process. Irrelevant measures, complicated design and data collection processes, rigid expectations, badly framed questions, mistimed reporting, and narrow frames of reference can distract your team from its work and distort the story of your accomplishments.

One of the practice challenges of the Human Systems Dynamics Institute over the past ten years has been to get the best out of an evaluation process while avoiding the ever-present pitfalls. As a social entrepreneurial organization, we evaluate our own work. As consultants to the private and public sectors, we support clients who evaluate their work and the work of others. As theory-based practitioners, we design and develop methods and models to support many different organizational functions, including systemic evaluation.

In this chapter, we look at three very different kinds of change and explore options for evaluating change in the most difficult, and also the most familiar, change environment.

THREE KINDS OF CHANGE

Human systems dynamics (HSD) draws on the physical sciences to understand and influence patterns in social systems. In particular, we turn models of complexity into methods of adaptive action for individuals, teams, organizations, and communities. Our work in evaluation depends on theories of change—both old and new.

Static change is the name we give to the oldest and simplest understanding of change. It assumes that a system is at rest before a change effort begins, that the change effort moves the system to a new place, and then it remains still again until it is disturbed by the next external force.

Everyone knows that human systems are never at rest, that no single force shifts a group of people to a new place, and that no change is so simple or permanent. Still, we have developed a way to think about and evaluate change in human systems as if it conformed to all the static assumptions. It is called outcome evaluation. The expectation is that a program or intervention will move the system from a defined and measurable initial state to a defined and measurable final state. The value and worth of the program can be determined based on its ability to shift the system from where it is to some other predefined position.

Though outcome evaluation never gives a complete picture of a change effort, it can give a very useful picture. It helps compare and contrast competing approaches in the same or similar circumstances. It helps establish a "return on investment" for the purposes of planning and resource management. It provides a sense of accomplishment as a program progresses. Outcome evaluation is good for many things, but it is not good for everything.

Dynamic change is the name we give to change that is more complex, but still predictable. Dynamic change assumes that once you start a change effort, it will continue in a predictable sequence to a predictable end. Based on Newtonian assumptions, this kind of change posits that when you know enough about the initial conditions of the system, and if you know all the forces acting on it, then you can predict every step of the path it will travel and where it will land in the end.

Everyone knows that no human change process travels a smooth and predictable path. We can never know all of the factors in the beginning nor anticipate all of the forces that may influence the change over time. Still, we have developed ways to think about and evaluate change in human organizations as if they were well behaved. Based on this assumption, we build logic models and track processes over time. We set milestones and judge performance against them. We expect to be able to replicate the course of change, even when we start in the most diverse situations and work with the most unknowable and variable environmental forces.

Again, judging change based on dynamic assumptions is not bad, it is just incomplete. Logic models and process evaluations are useful when the initial conditions and intervening forces are similar, even if they cannot be identical. They work for processes that have been tested and perfected over time or when the systemic variability can be held to a minimum. They work when the changes are small and when enough resources are available to counter any unexpected shift the environment introduces. In such circumstances, process evaluation works very well, but few social entrepreneurs are fortunate enough to work in such predictable and controllable environments.

The nonlinear sciences have opened the door to a third kind of change. We call it *dynamical change*, and it involves all of the strange and unpredictable phenomena associated with chaos and complexity sciences. Butterfly effects (small cause producing enormous effect), fractal patterns (spontaneous replication or reflection of patterns across scales from micro to macro), self-organized criticality (tipping point), and power law dynamics (small changes accumulate and trigger immense collapses) are all to be expected in the course of dynamical change. In short, a system can appear to be perfectly still, as tensions accumulate within or beyond it. At some unpredictable and critical point, the system shifts, and new patterns emerge across the system all at once.

Natural examples include earthquakes and avalanches, freezing and evaporation, ecological stability and species mutation. Human system examples are all around: the aha experience of learning, the conversion of crowd to mob, a cultural transformation, innovation, falling in love, psychotic breaks.

Dynamical change happens when a system is open to external influences that are too many or too variable to predict. Dynamical change happens when relationships change and affect the path and therefore the outcomes of change. Dynamical change happens when there are many or unknown relevant possibilities or when the possibilities are mutually interdependent. In other words, dynamical change happens when humans are involved in a change process because human systems are always open, high dimension, and nonlinear.

Change in human systems—individual, pair, team, organization, community—follows such unpredictable and uncontrollable paths; few evaluation disciplines have evolved to judge the value and worth of dynamical change.

EVALUATING DYNAMICAL CHANGE

In the past few years, professional evaluators have explored a variety of new models and methods that help them work with dynamical and systemic change. Iraj Imam and Bob Williams[1] brought together a wide range of systemic evaluation approaches, some of which accommodate dynamical change. In our practice, we have explored a variety of ways to evaluate change in unbounded, high dimension, and nonlinear systems. I will briefly describe five of those approaches here and refer you to other resources for the detailed models and methods for each.

1. *Adaptive action.* In HSD we use a simple learning model to support engagement in complex and dynamical change. It is called "adaptive action,"[2] and includes three key questions: What? So what? Now what?

We use these questions in an iterative process of continual engagement and assessment, where evaluation findings are immediately applied to decision-making and action. Michael Quinn Patton created developmental evaluation[3] to capture such patterns in dynamical change. Patton worked with Westley and Zimmerman[4] to explore stories of developmental evaluation in dynamical change. The approach they support involves thoughtful, iterative data collection, analysis, and action in which learning is both the method and the goal of evaluation activities.

2. *Storytelling.* Stories can capture the open, multidimensional, massively entangled patterns of dynamical change. Evaluation methods have been developed to capture and assess stories as evidence of change in complex and emergent systems.[5] Dave Snowden has developed a software application that analyzes microstories in a way that captures the patterns of the whole, the part, and the greater whole.[6] We collect stories through individual interviews, open-ended surveys, focus groups, and adaptive action experiments conducted by players in a system. In all of these cases, we find that the story creation and collection processes are as significant to the evaluation effort as the data analysis and reporting. By creating their stories, people across the system become more conscious of and more engaged with the dynamical changes that surround them.

3. *Participative evaluation.*[7] When change agents participate in the evaluation process, they are likely to capture the dynamical nature of the change, regardless of the kinds of data or approaches to data collection, analysis, and reporting. Participation takes many forms, and the level of participant engagement is determined by the use, context, and resources available for the evaluation process.[8]

4. *Complexity science models and methods.* Though the uses are not widespread or well documented, scholars and practitioners are beginning to draw ideas and methodologies directly from the complexity sciences.[9] In our experience, we have seen evaluations based on dynamical social network theory, nonlinear time series analysis and attractor reconstruction, Rene Thom's catastrophe theory, and the power law dynamics of self-organized criticality. Each of these is an experiment in itself, and many questions remain about theory and practice applying these tools that have been specifically designed to explore dynamical change. They hold great

promise as we build adaptive capacity and dynamical theory and practice into our profession.

5. *Conditions for self-organizing.* Much of the work of human systems dynamics is drawn from my research into the conditions for self-organizing.[10] We look for three conditions that are both the determinants and the indicators of pattern formation in complex adaptive systems. Containers hold the agents in a system together so they interact to form system-wide patterns. Differences articulate the pattern as well as establishing the tension that motivates change over time. Exchanges connect agents across differences and activate the potential energy held in the differences.

During dynamical change, both intentional and unintentional forces shift conditions in the system (the C, D, and E), and patterns of performance result. We have used the CDE model to evaluate change over time in complex systems in health care, social services, and agricultural research. Observing the conditions over time and from various points of view, we are able to characterize the system state in a way that captures the dynamical change over time and space without closing the system to outside influences, constraining the evaluation to a small number of indicators, or ignoring the nonlinear causality that shapes change in complex environments.

As social entrepreneurs, we thrive in systems that are open to opportunities, influenced by unknowable factors, and built upon mutual interdependencies. Outcome and process evaluations based on logic models and theories of change are useful, but their usefulness is limited in our complex environments. Old styles of evaluation are simply not sufficient to capture the value and worth of the dynamical changes we support in our work as social entrepreneurs. Complexity theory in general, and human systems dynamics in particular, offer a wide range of innovative ways to help us reap the benefits of rigorous evaluation without compromising the complexity that makes our work effective.

The field of dynamical evaluation is in its earliest stages of evolution, and the work of people like you will establish the models, methods, and approaches to help funders, partners, leaders, and whole communities build adaptive capacity and deal with the dynamical change of the unknown future we share.

NOTES

1. Bob Williams and Iraj Imam, *Systems Concepts in Evaluation: An Expert Anthology* (Point Reyes, CA: EdgePress of Inverness, 2007).
2. G. H. Eoyang and R. Holladay, *Getting Unstuck: Adaptive Action for the 21st Century* (San Francisco: Stanford University Press, in press).
3. Michael Quinn Patton, *Developmental Evaluation: Applying Complexity Concepts to Enhance Innovation and Use* (New York: Guilford Press, 2011).
4. F. Westley, Michael Quinn Patton, and B. Zimmerman, *Getting to Maybe: How the World is Changed* (Toronto: Random House Canada, 2006).
5. J. Dart, "A Dialogical, Story-Based Evaluation Tool: The Most Significant Change Technique," *American Journal of Evaluation*, 24(2) (2003): 137–155. doi: 10.1177/109821400302400202.
6. *SenseMaker*®. (n.d.). Retrieved from http://www.sensemaker-suite.com/.
7. G. Rowe and L. J. Frewer, "Public Participation Methods: A Framework for Evaluation," *Science, Technology & Human Values*, 25(1) (2000): 3–29. doi: 10.1177/016224390002500101.
8. A. Gregory, "Problematizing Participation: A Critical Review of Approaches to Participation in Evaluation Theory," *Evaluation*, 6(2) (2000): 179–199. doi: 10.1177/13563890022209208.
9. M. S. Poole, A. H. Van de Ven, K. Dooley, and M. E. Holmes, *Organizational Change and Innovation Processes: Theory and Methods for Research* (New York: Oxford University Press, 2000).
10. G. H. Eoyang, *Conditions for Self-Organizing in Human Systems,* Unpublished doctoral dissertation, The Union Institute and University, 2003.

Section 2

APPLICATION AND PRACTICE

Part 1

FINANCING THE WORLD: MICROFINANCE AND SOCIAL PROFIT

We create institutions and policies on the basis of the way we make assumptions about us and others. We accept the fact that we will always have poor people around us. So we have had poor people around us. If we had believed that poverty is unacceptable to us, and that it should not belong to a civilized society, we would have created appropriate institutions and policies to create a poverty-free world.

—Muhammad Yunus

WHEN GREED EXCEEDS PROTECTION, ECONOMIES crumble, societies become bankrupt, and history smirks at our repetition. One would think we would learn. The destructiveness of this model and the principle against which it is built hasn't slowed its spread over many failed attempts. Fortunately, there are other principles and models on which economies can grow, which neither exploit nor extort those they serve, and funny enough, can develop and sustain whole populations. It requires the removal of the need to produce vast wealth and replaces it with the idea of making enough wealth.

This is a worldwide struggle that has been going on for ages and has left billions at the point of starvation, and needlessly destroyed marketplaces that could support and maintain populations in some of the most verdant locations on earth. There is no question that harvesting the earth's resources sustains life on this planet—it feeds our families, provides good labor, and has led us to innovations that have helped build markets and industry. The model is spot-on until greed and vast wealth enter the equation.

William Foote and Root Capital had a different model in mind—bring people together to demonstrate the interdependence of the marketplace. Competition comes from the root—to strive with—not strive against. The whole reason competition came into being was to build markets, not dominate them. We are seeing that this model when properly administered and applied can succeed. It can bring people out of poverty, provide access to the necessities of life, and do so without having to take over the world.

At the forefront of the microfinance world is BRAC, founded by Sir Fazle Abed. BRAC originated in Bangladesh over 40 years ago and rivals Grameen in its worldwide reach and developmental support. Susan Davis, founder, CEO, and president of BRAC-USA, has operated at the leading edge of both Grameen and BRAC. She has also been at the center of the world of social entrepreneurship, leading the Ashoka Global Academy for Social Entrepreneurship as well as launching Ashoka efforts in countries around the world. Her work in the arena of microfinance and social entrepreneurship has been unparalleled in its dedication to fighting global poverty and the values that drive ethical opportunities for those seeking a better life for the marginalized and disadvantaged. As we see time and again, social entrepreneurial efforts are all about creating partnerships and collaboration. And the roots of the microfinance movement were no different. During her time in Dhaka, Bangladesh, she organized the Grameen Bank, BRAC, and Proshika donor consortia to scale up microfinance.

Microfinance is not alien to the United States. We have seen a similar model at work in financial institutions here in the United States. Our credit union system was originally designed as a neighbor helping neighbor approach, a means of getting around the exploitive banking systems that were emerging in the mid-1800s and coming to the aid of those folks who were doing the hard work that often supported the rest of the community.

Credit Unions were based on the idea of creating enough wealth, but not on producing windfall profits. So when Cliff Rosenthal took over the reins of the National Federation of Community Development Credit Unions, a subset of the credit union industry dedicated to serving low-income members, there was a clear understanding that the old models were not in place to serve the have-nots.

By creating financial cooperatives and providing markets for growers in Latin America and Africa, Root Capital has taken the sound principles of capital investment and infused once exploited farmers with a new model that recognizes their interdependence and realizes their ability to improve their lives. At its core, microfinance had its own roots in families helping each other and friends pitching in as well. Formalizing the process and then taking it global has begun to shift the entrenched pillars of a banking system that was never intended to serve the have-nots. BRAC was willing to seeing things differently, and the economies of the billions at the bottom have never been the same. In growing the CDCU system nearly fourfold and helping to initiate the Community Development Financial Institution system and establishing its accompanying CDFI Fund, Cliff Rosenthal has also shifted the model of how money reaches the marketplace and how people without means can still be served.

Our perspectives on money accumulation and utilization are a continual challenge for social entrepreneurs, who wrestle with the opportunity to create a new model capable of shifting hardship and strife and yet must still find a way to work with money to develop and continue their operations. Shifting our perceptions and our theories is just a place to start. Willy Foote and Cliff Rosenthal have applied this challenge on different continents and with growing success. They share an understanding of money and an understanding of the requirements of people in need. As we read through their chapters detailing how they reshaped their ideas of what was possible and initiated them to create and develop their organizations, we need to consider how we can apply similar approaches to the use of money that build on existing ideas and yet produce something both new and novel that can truly shift people out of poverty and produce enough wealth.

Chapter 8

CATALYZING GROWTH

William Foote
Root Capital

OUR FOUNDING STORY

In the late 1990s, I traded my job on Wall Street in Latin American corporate finance for a business journalism fellowship that took my wife and me on a two-year journey through Mexico. For the first time, I witnessed rural poverty. I also met many leaders in the countryside, often managers of agricultural businesses like farmer cooperatives, that had as much poise, sense of purpose, and leadership skills as any congressman or CEO.

The founding of Root Capital involves a specific cooperative of vanilla farmers I encountered in the Chimalapas jungle of southern Mexico. I remember my first visit—parrots chirping, a rushing river nearby, a forest canopy above. I also recall a sense of fear as the farmers were working hard to improve their livelihoods and struggling with drug traffickers operating in the jungle nearby. In the end, the vanilla cooperative failed, but it wasn't due to drug trafficking. It was because they lacked access to capital and markets and basic business skills they needed to succeed.

This vanilla association, like many other small and growing agricultural businesses, was stuck in what we call the "missing middle." Too big for microfinance, too small for the banks. So, I started thinking about how one might change that. A combination of intuition and impatience drove me down the road to Root Capital. Not long after I met the vanilla farmers, my wife and I were accepted into Harvard Business School. As we got in our truck and drove back to the United States, the experience of working with small-scale farmers was so fresh, and the immediacy of their need so acute, that I couldn't imagine doing anything else. I feared that if I didn't act on my ideas I would lose the sense of urgency. So, my wife went to Harvard and I founded what was to become Root Capital in 1999.

FROM VISION TO REALITY

Root Capital's mission is to grow rural prosperity by investing in agricultural businesses that build sustainable livelihoods in Africa and Latin America. These agricultural small and growing businesses (SGBs) connect farmers to markets, pay higher and more stable prices, serve as anchor institutions that deliver community benefits, and enable farmers to prosper.

Of the 2.6 billion people who survive on less than $2 per day, 75 percent live in rural areas. They are isolated from viable markets, and are relegated to a subsistence living that stresses the natural environment and makes it difficult for them to support their families.

Root Capital addresses the interrelated challenges of global poverty and environmental degradation by investing at the cross-section of two powerful forces for economic development:

- *Small and growing businesses:* SGBs create the majority of new jobs in developed countries but, due to limited access to capital, account for only a sliver of the economy in developing countries.
- *Agriculture:* The World Bank estimates that growth in the agricultural sector is twice as effective in reducing poverty as growth in any other sector.

Root Capital has a three-pronged strategy: finance, advise, and catalyze. The "finance" and "advise" strategies work together to extend the capital and financial management training that rural SGBs need to grow.

FINANCE

First and foremost, Root Capital is an impact-focused agricultural lender. Through our "finance" strategy, we seek to demonstrate a scalable and sustainable business model to serve agricultural SGBs.

Through our Sustainable Trade Fund, we extend capital to agricultural businesses that lack financing, support them with pre- and postinvestment financial management training, and accompany their growth over time with larger loans and more financial products. The success of our clients propels our own as revenue from more mature clients funds loans to earlier stage businesses that lack access to finance. At an aggregate level, a growing and financially sustainable portfolio enables us to demonstrate the financial and impact opportunity and attracts capital from investors and inspires replication by peers and partners.

We also strive to push the frontier of rural finance where others have yet to tread. Through our Frontier Portfolios, we innovate to reach a broader range of the five hundred million farm families who live in poverty, including farmers who grow staple crops for domestic consumption rather than high-value cash crops for export.

For instance, Freshco is a Kenyan company that sells high-yield, drought-resistant seed, especially maize, to small-scale farmers. Maize production is essential to Kenya's fragile food security, but droughts in recent years have devastated harvests. By providing better seed to Kenyan farmers, Freshco is helping to feed a nation in which nearly three million people don't have enough to eat. Freshco doubled production of its 11 varieties of maize seed last year with Root Capital financing.

ADVISE

In our experience lending to rural SGBs, we have seen that capital alone is often not enough to unlock businesses' potential for growing rural prosperity. For example, Ankole is an association of 3,700 small-scale coffee farmers in the tropical forests of Southwestern Uganda. Ankole initially sold its product through local middlemen because it lacked the capital and management capacity needed to work directly with international buyers. Root Capital spent four days onsite working with Ankole's team to develop a system of tracking coffee stocks, recording transactions, and managing cash flow.

With those basic tools in place, Root Capital approved a $113,000 loan. Ankole used the funds to purchase coffee from its farmers and it received a price premium by working directly with the end-buyer. Just seven months later, Ankole paid down the loan in full and used some of the earnings to purchase computers and to hire an accountant to manage its books.

Root Capital began developing its Financial Advisory Services capacity in 2006 to deliver financial training to rural enterprises. Since then, we have successfully strengthened the financial management capacity of nearly one hundred agricultural businesses. These engagements have confirmed that rural business leaders, when equipped with sound financial management practices and processes, are better positioned to access credit, compete in the marketplace, grow their enterprises, and support improved livelihoods for small-scale farmers and their families.

CATALYZE

Because we barely scratch the surface of agricultural lending demand in developing countries, Root Capital seeks to stimulate others to adopt our value chain finance innovations. The "missing middle"—the gap between microfinance and commercial banking—is so vast that even if we exceed our growth targets, we will meet only a fraction of the need. We aspire to do more than simply grow our direct lending and financial training. We aim for the impact, scale, and financial sustainability of our lending to create a demonstration effect that attracts new capital from existing and new financiers to serve the SGBs we cannot reach ourselves, and to do so in a way that promotes sustainable, social, and environmental practices.

Our "catalyze" strategy has two parts:

- *Innovate:* We conduct internal R&D to seed new business areas, document our impact at the household and business levels, and foster continuous improvement in our operations and increase our impact.
- *Accelerate:* We share tools and learning from our work and engage like-minded peers to build the infrastructure of common standards, impact metrics, and responsible lending practices necessary for the industry to thrive and scale.

SUSTAINING GROWTH

Over the past decade, we have disbursed more than $368 million in credit to 360 SGBs in Africa and Latin America. By 2016, we will have tripled our loan portfolio to $190 million financing to 650 businesses, reaching over 2 million small-scale farming households and nearly 11 million people, while playing a leadership role in catalyzing a market to serve tens of millions more.

As we scale our impact, we see three critical areas:

Talent. The hardest part of building an organization is attracting, training, and retaining talent. Operationally, over the next five years, we will move toward regionalization and decentralization. This will substantially increase decision-making capabilities and responsibilities in the field. We need people with both hardcore financial and technical skills and with deeply rooted social and environmental commitments. We've learned the hard way that it's much easier to teach the hard skills than to teach passion, intuition, empathy, or values.

Process. In the past few years, one of the biggest challenges for Root Capital has been *honing the systems and processes* that enable us to serve rural businesses more efficiently and that make our model more compelling to would-be adopters. For example, we have spent a lot of time, adapting the risk classification system of the Office of the Controller of the Currency to guide all our credit scoring efforts, and thus create a more off-the-shelf banking product for financial institutions to adopt. This is not sexy work, but it is critical.

Culture. I have been amazed by the importance of culture in an organization seeking to have impact at scale. We serve agricultural businesses, and we are also a small and growing business ourselves. The small part is fine, but the growing part poses real challenges, including the risk of losing a common culture—as generalists are superseded by functional experts and emails rival face-to-face conversations.

BEYOND THE SOCIAL ENTREPRENEUR

Whether it's through music or other team connections, creating a common culture may fill a fissure that we're feeling right now in the "social enterprise" industry. In Root Capital's case, we have grown beyond the vision of a single individual. Our work now represents the collective vision of more than one hundred talented professionals spread across offices in nine countries. Similarly, many of the enterprises founded by early social entrepreneurs are now realized well beyond the scope of their charismatic founders.

As industry players expand, now more than ever we feel a need for connectedness, cohesion, and definition. With all the bottom lines to which we collectively manage, and in an undeniably uncertain environment, we need a shared moral compass. Social enterprise is still so young that there is no clear "best practice" for what we should be doing; no well-established playbook with rules and procedures.

We sometimes struggle and that's good. We need creativity and flexibility to attack the problems we attempt to fix, yet we need the structure that will help us all collectively achieve our goals. For now, I think the best that we can hope for is a common set of values and a shared culture. These will serve as our guide, our North Star, as we pursue scattered solutions to the world's most complex problems.

Chapter 9

SEEDING THE ROOTS OF MICROFINANCE

Susan Davis
BRAC-USA

PIONEERING MICROFINANCE

The singularly remarkable story of BRAC, a global development organization based in Bangladesh that is by most measures the world's largest nongovernmental organization, serves as a powerful illustration of what determined social entrepreneurs can do using microfinance as a springboard for social change. Founded in 1972 during the first days of Bangladeshi independence by a former oil company accountant named Fazle Hasan Abed, the organization had its origins in a relatively small effort to provide relief in the aftermath of the 1970 Bhola cyclone. That storm was a disaster of staggering magnitude, killing up to five hundred thousand people; worse still, it was followed by the War of Liberation between West Pakistan and the ethnic Bengali parts of East Pakistan, now Bangladesh.

When the fledgling Bangladesh declared independence in 1971, many saw it as a place bereft of hope, seemingly cursed by geography, circumstance, and intractable poverty. Today, despite facing challenges such as poor governance, frequent flooding, and the world's highest population density among larger countries, the country has made startling gains, including a 75 percent reduction in maternal and infant mortality. Development scholars say it is partly due to a robust civil society, including BRAC, which is now the largest nonstate employer in Bangladesh. Paul Collier, author of *The Bottom Billion*,[1] has called BRAC "the most astounding social enterprise in the world." The organization's story is one of growth, innovation, and tenacity that any aspiring social entrepreneur would do well to follow.

As Abed, now Sir Fazle Hasan Abed since his knighthood by the British crown in 2010, said on the occasion of BRAC's fortieth anniversary in February 2012:

> At the time of our independence, our health indicators were some of the worst in the world. Today, the progress we have made is the envy of most of the developing nations in South Asia and beyond. In these last 40 years, infant mortality in Bangladesh has come down from 200 to less than 50, maternal mortality from 800 to less than 200, and average life expectancy at birth has risen from 40 to 65. Fertility, which was as high as 6.5 [children per woman] in 1972, has fallen to 2.7. While it is true that no single organization can take credit for this amazing turnaround, we at BRAC can nevertheless take great pride in the role that we have played in support of governmental efforts to bringing about these successes.

The full story of BRAC is recounted in Ian Smillie's biography of the organization, *Freedom from Want*.[2] The first BRAC project was a limited effort to provide clothing, shelter, and livelihood in a remote area of northern Bangladesh called Sulla, funded by a grant from Oxfam. As Smillie recounts, by the time the project had finished, the founder and those around him—readers of the pedagogical theories of Frantz Fanon and Paulo Freire, advocating education as means of "conscientization" of powerless members of society—were already starting to envision something much larger:

> Abed had seen BRAC as a temporary phenomenon, something that might last a year or so. After the emergency had passed, it would disband, and he would start to look for a job. He asked the people who had worked with him in Sulla what they thought. All had seen the area's deep-seated poverty, and

all knew their relief and reconstruction efforts had only touched the surface of the need. All had begun to see that there was a real opportunity for an organization like BRAC to make a lasting difference, but it would require more time and more money.

BRAC is now active in ten countries. Originally an acronym for Bangladesh Rehabilitation Assistance Committee (later Bangladesh Rural Advancement Committee), the organization is now formally known simply as BRAC. With 125,000 paid employees and 150,000 BRAC-affiliated microfranchised entrepreneurs, it has an estimated reach of 138 million people. In Bangladesh, where it touches the lives of an estimated 110 million of a total population of about 160 million, close to 70 percent of the organization budget is generated from its own activities, which include microfinance, textiles, mainstream banking, a dairy business with 20–30 percent market share, high-yield seed distribution for farmers, and over 100,000 community health workers providing vital healthcare goods and services to their neighbors. But the vision remains the same as in the early days, "an ideal of a world free from all forms of exploitation and discrimination," as Sir Fazle said at his acceptance of the WISE Prize for Education in Qatar in 2011.

ENLARGING THE SCALE: MOVING BEYOND BANGLADESH

Arguably the most interesting part of BRAC's story over the last ten years— indeed, perhaps one of the most engaging ongoing stories in international development, period—is the expansion of BRAC's services outside its native Bangladesh, starting in 2002, when it sent its first brave team into post-war Afghanistan. With the return of refugees after the fall of the Taliban regime, BRAC saw similarities with its own experience in Bangladesh in the early 1970s. It wanted to see whether its approaches might work in a foreign context. Today, BRAC is active in ten countries, including five in Africa. One of its fastest scale-ups is taking place in Uganda, another country emerging from its own history of entrenched poverty, discrimination against women, violence, and displacement. BRAC's experience in Uganda serves as a case study of an approach to serving the poor that it calls "microfinance multiplied."

Using BRAC's experience in Uganda, the organization has gone into partnership with The MasterCard Foundation, a relatively new philanthropy based in Toronto, Canada, to scale up the microfinance multiplied approach. The MasterCard Foundation has recognized BRAC's solution: an approach born in the global South, with programs built around adaptations of BRAC's tactics in defeating poverty in Bangladesh over 40 years. Thanks to the partnership between these two organizations, BRAC Uganda has grown quickly to become the largest nongovernmental organization in the country. The organization is effectively trying to compress 40 years of development in Bangladesh into 5–10 years, with a massive scale-up from 2006, when it started from scratch, to 2011, when it ended the year with 105 branches, 1,830 employees, over 100,000 borrowers, and a $15 million loan portfolio. It has a total estimated reach of 2 million people in Uganda and is on track to reach 4.2 million, or about 12 percent of the country, by 2016. Rigorous reporting requirements work to the benefit of both sides of the BRAC-MasterCard Foundation partnership, which is seen as more than just a financial commitment, but a collaborative learning venture, or "knowledge partnership," whose goal is to build an evidence base for development approaches to microfinance and youth learning that can be adapted and scaled up on a South-South axis.

BRAC's microfinance multiplied approach is based on the premise that microborrowing is merely a starting point for individual empowerment and community development. Women especially can reap exponential benefits from microfinance when it is combined with a package of interventions that touch multiple points on several value chains, including the educational value chain that begins with free primary education, extends into the financial and social empowerment of teenage girls (including the ability to take small loans), and continues with lifelong learning. At the center of this model are groups of women that meet weekly with a BRAC community organizer or loan officer who disburses loans and collects repayments. These groups are the primary distribution channel for technical assistance to their communities. For example, BRAC trains some women to become model farmers, who in turn teach good farming practices to other members of their village. Other group members are trained as health promoters who share their knowledge and sell vital health care goods and services to their neighbors.

The microfinance multiplied approach includes livelihood training, microfranchised entrepreneurship creation (sometimes called a "business in a box" approach), and the piloting of new financial products for agriculture, poultry, livestock, and even school fees. BRAC's alternative primary schools are especially vital in postconflict northern Uganda, where refugees from the rebellion of the Lord's Resistance Army have been returning home from internally displaced persons (IDP) camps since fighting there ended in 2006. As is standard procedure for BRAC, all of these pilots are rigorously tested to assess the viability of new products and ventures before they are launched nationwide.

LEARNING THE LESSONS TO FINANCE THE POOR

BRAC's Uganda experience shows how an organization, one for whom the values of social enterprise are built into its DNA, can scale up microfinance services in a new cultural context. The BRAC experience points to a number of lessons for aspiring microfinance institutions seeking to deliver social returns by offering financial services to the poor.

First, think big. The key to understanding BRAC's approach to poverty alleviation is the oft-repeated quotation from its founder, Sir Fazle Hasan Abed: "Small may be beautiful, but big is sometimes necessary." The BRAC approach to scaling up microfinance and microfinance-related activities is driven by two factors. The first is the sheer urgency of the problem: As of 2008, 1.4 billion people lived on less than $1.25 a day, according to World Bank estimates; BRAC sees its experience in Bangladesh as an opportunity to provide immediate assistance by bringing tested solutions to the doorsteps of the world's poorest. A second factor, one sometimes overlooked, is the efficiencies brought about by operating at scale. The poor need access to capital at reasonable rates, but economies of scale are often the only way to make microfinance affordable for the poor on a self-sustaining basis. Subsidized or artificially low interest rates are likely to prove unsustainable without plans to grow quickly; institutions interested in limiting their reach to a handful of branches might therefore look into partnering with a larger organization.

Second, think beyond lending. Savings accounts in particular are proving an increasingly useful tool for providing financial stability to the poor. Aspiring social entrepreneurs in the finance sector should provide for savings accounts alongside credit, for both are vital tools in creating freedom and opportunity for the poor.

Third, start young and invest in girls. Social entrepreneurs cannot afford to ignore the burgeoning youth demographic in large parts of the developing world, especially Africa. Members of BRAC's girls' clubs learn the importance of savings at an early age, and many take loans while still teenagers. Social entrepreneurs should work closely with youth, girls especially, to determine how access to financial products can assist with their actual needs and future aspirations.

Finally, beware of overborrowing. BRAC has been known for novel methods of due diligence. Loan officers have been known to ask borrowers' children whether their parents attend other microfinance meetings in addition to BRAC's, for instance. Such caution is necessary to avoid over-indebtedness, which is counterproductive to the social goals of microlending. The microfinance crisis in the Indian state of Andhra Pradesh in 2010 shows what can happen when loan portfolios grow too fast. Microfinance institutions have a responsibly for preventing an overheated microfinance market, which can lead to borrowers overextending themselves. Such a scenario creates not greater freedom and opportunity, but their exact opposites.

The BRAC playbook, boiled down to a few simple rules, might look something like this: monitor, evaluate, adapt, perfect, and then scale up. BRAC is famous for applying strict internal controls. Accounting on the field level is monitored by a team of internal evaluators, and the organization holds to a zero tolerance policy if it encounters corruption among its ranks. The organization also adapts where necessary. Dating back to its first microloans in the 1970s, BRAC recognized that providing access to capital would only bring down one of many barriers standing in the way of those seeking to lift themselves out of poverty. Small loans would not, by themselves, provide enough opportunity on a widespread basis to allow large numbers of the poor to begin climbing the economic ladder. In Uganda, the organization reacted to a new economic and cultural context and a different set of market demands by placing renewed emphasis on livelihood development, which lies at the core of its "microfinance multiplied" approach to development. After making the adaptations needed to best serve local communities, BRAC takes a business-minded approach, perfecting its processes through routinization and making them easily replicated. It's an approach that has served the organization well over 40 years, from its humble beginnings in Bangladesh to its massive scale today—a movement of hundreds of thousands of empowered, like-minded individuals bringing solutions to the doorsteps of millions.

NOTES

1. Paul Collier, *The Bottom Billion* (USA: Oxford University Press, 2008).
2. Ian Smillie, *Freedom from Want* (Kumarian Press, 2009).

Chapter 10

THE FINANCIAL COOPERATIVE MOVEMENT

Clifford Rosenthal[*]
National Federation of Community
Development Credit Unions

FINDING COOPERATIVISM

Coming of age in the late 1960s in the United States meant questioning the established order. For some of us, angry rejection of the war against Vietnam led to a reinterpretation of the world; like others of my generation, I came to see political conflict as an expression of the drive for corporate, capitalist domination.

As the Vietnam War was gradually, painfully winding down, another crisis began to attract my attention: world hunger, perpetuated and exacerbated by corporate domination of the food production and distribution chain. I took a small, local step, aimed at eliminating some of the middlemen in the chain, organizing my neighbors in New York City, rewarding our collective efforts with tangible economic benefits—and at the same time, educating people about the nature of the world food system. I organized a food-buying cooperative.

Throughout the 1970s, I worked to bring this notion of cooperative empowerment to low-income and minority communities in the United States—first in the successive urban neighborhoods where I lived, then working as a co-op organizer for a Native American consortium in the state of Connecticut, later as a technical assistance specialist for a national organization serving migrant and seasonal farmworkers.

It was at this organization in Washington, DC that I first became acquainted with credit unions—financial cooperatives that pool the funds of individuals to lend to each other. Often, I describe this encounter in 1979 as love at first sight. Credit unions seemed to me the highest, and most productive, expression of collective empowerment, a step—especially for low-income people—toward controlling their economic lives. Most compelling to me was the fact that credit unions in the United States had a history dating to the first decade of the twentieth century: credit unions were *sustainable* cooperatives that survived numerous business cycles, including the Great Depression of the 1930s.

REBUILDING THE FEDERATION

It was at this time that I discovered the National Federation of Community Development Credit Unions, an association of credit unions that focused entirely on low-income and minority communities, urban, rural, and reservation-based. The federation was (and is) a nonprofit charity—a nongovernmental organization, or NGO—that at the same time was a membership organization, uniting scores of local cooperatives with the common mission of fighting poverty. The federation spoke to both my core philosophic values and my personal motivation. It was based on a vision of self-help, of independent communities empowering themselves through cooperation, rather than top-down charismatic leadership. But it also was an actor in the national arena.

I came to the federation in 1980, anticipating a stimulating midlevel career, running training programs under the leadership of a CEO whose commitment and talents I admired. And for a year, my plans were on track. But the federation's business model was fatally flawed: literally, 99 percent of its budget came from federal funding from one agency, with dues accounting for the rest. The Reagan administration quickly began to abolish funding and—they hoped—dismantle the national infrastructure for organizations serving the poor. By the winter of 1982–83, the federation was left with a scant $5,000 in dues and a rapidly shrinking membership. By April 1983, its CEO announced that he could no longer sustain the organization. And the chairman reluctantly declared that the organization—founded in 1974 by a small band of dedicated antipoverty crusaders—had enjoyed a good run, but there were no resources to continue its existence.

It was at that moment that my career as a social entrepreneur began in earnest. I offered to run the organization without pay (thanks to a fellowship I received from Columbia University) on the sole condition that I be given the title of executive director. My terms were accepted.

For about a year, I operated the organization out of a study in my house, armed with an answering machine and early versions of the personal computer. In the fall of 1983, I added a second person part-time—an African American woman who was one of the first to manage a credit union in the Deep South, and who had served in the federal regulatory agency.

I took away one obvious but compelling lesson from the crisis of the federation: an organization or enterprise should never be dependent on one revenue source. The federal government was an inconstant ally and supporter. Diversification of funding was crucial. The leadership of the federation had taken the first step by developing a vision for a Capitalization Program for our member community development credit unions: the federation would borrow from national foundations, banks, and others and reinvest in credit unions, earning a small margin or spread to cover operating costs. My task was to use this and other mechanisms to rebuild the federation from a position of literal bankruptcy.

An important opportunity presented itself in New York City, where we are based. The money-center banks that dominated the retail banking scene were withdrawing from low-income areas, eliminating branches and services. There was considerable concern in public policy circles about the gaps that were created: Who, or what, would fill them? I began making the case in forums of regulatory agencies and others that credit unions would be the "wave of the future" for low-income communities, providing affordable loans and savings products where large banks could not or would not. The idea had considerable appeal to policymakers and philanthropies. But credit unions were relatively unknown as a tool for social policy, and their track record was scanty.

The challenge was proof of concept: we needed a visible demonstration of why this unlikely idea of low-income people banding together to do what multibillion-dollar banks could not would work. The opportunity came when a major bank announced plans to close the last branch serving "Alphabet City" on Manhattan's Lower East Side. No bank came forward to take its place. So, I began working with local community activists to organize a credit union. The 18-month process, aided by regulatory persuasion and a major community organizing effort, culminated in the opening of the Lower East Side People's Federal Credit Union on May 1, 1986. (In 2011, it celebrated its twenty-fifth anniversary as a $30-million, fully self-sufficient credit union providing "lifeline" banking services to thousands of people.)

Armed with the example of the Lower East Side credit union, I began to actively market the concept to the philanthropic, banking, and social investment worlds. Faced with an inhospitable national political environment, I rebuilt the organization on the chassis of a New York effort, tapping local sources for local projects that in turn subsidized our national work. We won contracts for job training and housing-related financing. But most important: our key strategy for mobilizing funds nationally began to expand, our Capitalization Program.

In the mid-1980s, we began to raise significant amounts of debt, initially from religious investors, then from foundations. Starting with a modest loan of $30,000 in 1982 from a Catholic women's order, by the end of the decade we managed several millions of dollars from prominent national foundations, denominations, and banks. We reinvested those funds at a margin and generated a growing, if not huge, stream of nongrant earned income to support our programs.

By 1990, our membership of credit unions had doubled, to about one hundred. We had some momentum. But our financial situation was precarious.

Several years earlier, I had developed the concept for a national fund to support institutions like credit unions that provided loans in low-income communities. In the early 1990s, I was able to engage other organizations in a coalition to press this idea. In 1992, Bill Clinton won his first term as president—after campaigning with a call for a network of "community development banks." With a powerful champion in the White House, we were able to work successfully for the creation of the federal Community

Development Financial Institutions (CDFI) Fund. Opening its doors in 1995, by 2011 it had provided permanent capital to hundreds of CDFIs, including community development credit unions and loan funds, totaling more than $1 billion. "CDFI" became a valued brand and, increasingly, the federal government's vehicle of choice for rolling out new initiatives aimed at addressing socioeconomic problems.

Along with scores of our member credit unions, the federation won valuable investments from the CDFI Fund. Primarily in the form of grants, these funds have been crucial to our expansion. In 2011, our Capitalization Program—now known as the Community Development Investment Program—managed $50 million and included a secondary market for purchasing affordable mortgage loans. Our net worth was approaching $10 million—capital that we vitally needed to continue our mission of investing in mission-driven credit unions in economically vulnerable communities.

SUSTAINING OUR MISSION AND OUR ENTERPRISE

There are various national intermediaries in the United States that channel capital into low-income communities. Only one, the National Federation of Community Development Credit Unions, has a governance structure that is accountable to those communities. The federation is governed by an uncompensated, elected board composed of the managers and volunteers of low-income communities themselves. It is the most ethnically and racially diverse board of its kind, and the one most in tune with local concerns. Our governance keeps us true to our mission.

The complexity of the federation—as membership organization, as a publicly supported charity, as a financial intermediary, and as a source of technical expertise for hire—is an asset in this environment. Our funding mix will change. But the adaptability we have had to develop over more than 30 years bodes well for our ability to survive in a difficult global economic environment.

NOTE

*Clifford Rosenthal stepped down from the National Federation of Community Development Credit Unions after 32 years in May 2012 to assume a position in a new federal agency charged with consumer protection.

Part 2

INTERACTION, COLLABORATION, AND POSITIVELY DISRUPTIVE SOLUTIONS

It is the long history of humankind (and animal kind, too) those who learned to collaborate and improvise most effectively have prevailed.
—Charles Darwin

ONE OF THE GREATEST IMPEDIMENTS TO SOCIAL entrepreneurial success is the belief that "I can do it myself." We see it time and again in the proliferation of nonprofit organizations that are all designed to address the same issue, that all claim to have the right answer, and who are all going after the same dwindling resources. The idea of sharing capacities, as a way to lower costs, is lost within the overarching egos of these founders who have the right answer. Working together in the nonprofit world is nice to talk about, but real collaboration to actually collectively solve problems has been slow to evolve because of the fear of having to also share funding. Collaboration is alright in theory, but stay away from my donor base!

Collaboration is about deliberately creating interactions, out of which, we hope, something positive will emerge. It does not have to happen that way. Unfortunately, the properties of emergence are not contingent on the ingredient mix. That is the nature of complex living systems. We operate in this fluid environment in which all we can really do is provide the space for things to take place and then explain what happened. But it is precisely because of this unpredictable nature that collaboration yields what it does. When you and I bring our whole chain of individual experience to this moment and interact to solve a common problem, both our lives are changed going forward. It is the very nature of the process. That moment was both informed and influenced by what each of us brought to it. But what we walk away from it with was what we cocreated.

If what we, as social entrepreneurs, do is actualize deliberate disruptive designs as a way of shifting intransigent social issues, then it stands to reason that the means for making this work effectively is collaboration. Todd Khozein, Michael Karlberg, and Carrie Freeman demonstrate and present in their own collaborative style how and why shifting entrepreneurship from a traditional competitive model to one of interdependent collaboration provides an avenue for successful social entrepreneurship. Competition is one of those often misunderstood terms that carries a lot of heat and emotion with it, especially in the social entrepreneurial world. However, its original meaning is "to strive with," as opposed to its current iteration of "striving against." Khozein et al. show that the real emergent power of social entrepreneurial efforts comes from a collaborative striving with. Interestingly, too, from an economic perspective, competition is how markets get built, as opposed to the monopolistic inspired vision of domination of market share. Through real collaboration, the ideas and reasoning on which the marketplace for social entrepreneurial efforts can develop and proliferate become apparent. Contrary to the image of Davy Crockett's Rugged Individualist—by way of the philosopher John Locke—as long as we are a social world based on striving against, our ability to create a healthy economy and marketplace is vastly diminished.

The notion of collaboration is about establishing a place to find common ground out of which we can create new opportunities. When Greg Wendt and his colleagues established the Green Business Networking events, they did so without expectation of what would emerge. All they did was provide common ground, and brought together those who self-selected into the mix.

The beauty of the monthly event was that one never knew who would be there. The purpose was to just show up and interact, to network. The only thing you really knew was that the people who would show up with you were interested in Green Business. The continuing success of the events is based on providing space for the interaction. Self-organization only succeeds within a bounded environment. The extension of these informal events was a more formal gathering, the Green Economy Think Tank Day. At this day-long event, Wendt and his colleagues would attract a hundred people or so, provide them with preselected topic areas required to create a local Green Economy, and let the discussion ensue. The ideas generated within these discussions would then be presented to the group as a whole, and then using a unique electronic capturing system, would be voted on as to value, appeal, and interest. Those tabulations, almost instant market research, would then direct the work of those self-selected units with what was considered the most effective approaches to creating the local Green Economy. From its founding roots in Los Angeles and Santa Monica, Green Economy Think Tank Days have spread to San Francisco, New Orleans, and out across the country: deliberate collaboration to surface the next disruption.

The important factor within all collaboration is capturing what emerges out of the interaction and putting it into action. If we don't apply what we learn from what takes place within our collaborations, then we might as well be talking to a wall. But working together is not just about finding a place on which we can all agree. Agreement is actually not what we are looking for, because for us to agree there is acceptance that something right is being agreed upon. This kind of an interaction is based on opinion and ultimately ego. What we are looking for within our collaborations is alignment, our ability to move forward from common ground. Alignment is based on mutuality. To effectively tackle the challenges we as social entrepreneurs take on, the key is found within alignment. Whenever there is a disagreement, we can return to what we are aligned around, our common ground, and from there move forward. It is generally accepted that we can't do this work alone. If that is so, it requires us to learn to work together to not simply create more "yap," but to create a positive disruption to the work that hasn't met its objectives, and to design together the next innovation that actually will get the job done.

Chapter 11

FROM COMPETITION TO COLLABORATION: TOWARD A NEW FRAMEWORK FOR ENTREPRENEURSHIP

Todd Khozein, Michael Karlberg, and Carrie Freeman
SecondMuse

WE CANNOT SOLVE THE PROBLEMS FACING humanity today within the same conceptual framework that created those problems. If social entrepreneurs hope to make a significant contribution to the betterment of the world, they will not only need to address significant social and environmental problems with creative business plans, they will also need to contribute to the emergence of a new, more adaptive, conceptual framework for economic activity. In other words, social entrepreneurship ultimately must be about the reinvention of the business itself. (What Craig Dunn has referred to as "deliberate disruptive design.") Otherwise, social and ecological problems will continue to proliferate faster than social entrepreneurs can ever hope to respond.

At the core of this emerging design framework must be a more mature and holistic conception of human nature; a corresponding reconceptualization of social and economic relationships; and a recognition that the increasingly complex problems facing humanity today can only be solved through sustained, effective, and altruistically motivated collaboration among people and organizations who bring diverse insights, experiences, talents, and capacities to bear on those problems. This chapter explores several foundational elements of such a framework and then briefly discusses the experience of one entrepreneurial effort—SecondMuse—that illustrates initial efforts to apply this framework in a learning mode.

FROM SELF-INTERESTED COMPETITION TO ORGANIC COLLABORATION

Prevailing conceptions of human nature—especially in the fields of business and economics—often reduce human beings down to our basest material instincts and appetites. "Homo economicus" is thus frequently understood as a competitive, egoistic, and self-maximizing creature engaged in rational calculations designed to maximize its material well-being.

This caricature of human nature exaggerates some features of our nature while obscuring others. Most notably, it obscures our capacity for cooperation, altruism, and sacrifice for the common good. In this regard, all of the human sciences are beginning to demonstrate that humans embody the dual potential for competition or cooperation, egoism or altruism, self-interested orientations and other-interest orientations.[1] Which of these potentials is more fully developed depends on a complex interplay among our education and training, our social environment, the institutional incentive structures we operate within, and the personal choices we make as we navigate these systems.

A growing number of thoughtful entrepreneurs, economists, and others are adopting this more holistic view of human nature. Yet, on the whole, business practices and economic policies continue to implicitly reflect the assumption that human beings are essentially selfish. Based on this assumption, the dynamics of self-interested competition are widely presumed to be natural, inevitable, or even ideal expressions of human nature. Competitive relations are thus assumed to be the normal operating mode of entrepreneurs, corporations, governmental agencies, and even nation-states. Accordingly, our market systems, our political systems, our legal systems, our educational systems, and even many forms of recreation and leisure have all been structured in ways that incentivize and reinforce competitive relationships, thus cultivating our basest instincts and appetites rather than our noblest talents and capacities.

The "culture of contest" that results from this is becoming increasingly maladaptive in an age of ever-increasing social and ecological interdependence.[2] These maladaptive consequences can be seen in the growing disparities of wealth and poverty within and between most nation-states, and in the social conflict and instability that results. These consequences can also be seen in the mounting ecological crises that stem from a global race to liquidate the earth's ecological capital in the name of self-interested, short-term, material acquisition. And finally, these consequences can be seen in the growing epidemic of alienation, depression, and anomy that characterize the most competitive societies today.

In order to move beyond the prevailing culture of contest and create a more just and sustainable social order, we need to critically reexamine the concept of *competition* itself. Competition, as the term is widely used today, tends to conflate two distinct sets of ideas that need to be disentangled. When people use the word "competition," they are often referring, simultaneously, to (a) the pursuit of excellence, innovation, and the establishment and productivity within a market system; and (b) the self-interested pursuit of mutually exclusive gains, with resultant winners and losers.

The problem with conflating these two sets of ideas is that there is no necessary correspondence between a and b. Indeed, self-interested competition can actually undermine excellence, innovation, and productivity.[3] Moreover, while self-interest can clearly be a motivating force in human behavior, other motives can be just as powerful, if not more so. These other deep wells of motivation include the *intrinsic* rewards that come from the pursuit of excellence, innovation, and productivity. They also include the motivation to contribute to the betterment of the world, to enact a higher meaning and purpose in one's life, or to make material sacrifices for a higher cause. Indeed, throughout history, many people have been motivated to give their time, their energy, and in some cases their lives for an ennobling purpose or cause. In contrast, where is the self-interested actor who has tapped into equivalent sources of motivation in the name of competitive acquisition?

Once we disaggregate conventional notions of competition in this way, we can see that the most valuable aspects of "competition"—the pursuit of excellence, innovation, and productivity—are not contingent on self-interested behaviors, and they need not result in winners or losers. On the contrary, they assume their most mature form within a framework of cooperation and mutual gains—or a framework of collaboration.

Collaboration, as we are using the term, refers to cooperation among diverse individuals, groups, or organizations working together systematically to achieve a common goal. In recent years, significant attention has been paid to the development of more effective collaboration among diverse individuals or entities within organizations. However, such intraorganizational collaboration is often encouraged merely to enable an organization to compete more effectively against other organizations for access to scarce resources, markets, profits, and so forth. Likewise, some attention has also been paid to interorganizational collaboration, but largely for the same reasons: to enable partner organizations to compete more effectively against rivals in zero-sum relationships. Collaboration, in other words, is still widely viewed as a strategy of self-interested competition.

Unfortunately, this self-interested view of collaboration is part of the same conceptual framework, alluded to earlier, that is becoming deeply maladaptive under today's conditions of ever-increasing social and ecological interdependence. Under these conditions, the well-being of every individual and group is increasingly dependent on the well-being of the entire social body. These new conditions therefore require us to adopt a more mature conception of social and economic relationships. Rather than viewing society as an arena for self-interested competition, we need to begin viewing it as a complex living system—or an organic whole. In other worlds, we need to reframe our conception of society by shifting from a *social contest* frame to a *social body* frame.[4]

Within any healthy organic body, relations among its component cells and organs are characterized by collaboration and reciprocity—not competition. Indeed, within an organic body, the competitive hoarding of resources or the pursuit of mutually exclusive gains is a sure sign of disease. Yet these dysfunctional relations continue to dominant human societies—especially within market interactions.

In this context, we believe that collaborative dynamics—in the organic sense of the term—must increasingly characterize human relations at all levels of society, including market relations. Collaboration, in this sense, is characterized by diverse organizations working together systematically toward goals that benefit the entire social body.

There is clearly much to learn about how market relations can be characterized by organic forms of interorganizational collaboration, motivated by concern for the entire social body. In the contemporary world there are few existing models to study because the entire framework of market interaction today tends to incentivize self-interested competition. In this context, the authors of this chapter, along with a growing group of associates, have dedicated themselves to a process of systematic and applied learning along these lines, within the evolving conceptual framework of a learning community called the Harmony Equity Group, of which they are members. One of the enterprises that has emerged from this learning community is SecondMuse, which is pioneering new models of organic collaboration that are bringing diverse private-sector and public-sector organizations together in projects that contribute to the betterment of society.

ORGANIC COLLABORATION AS AN EVOLUTIONARY IMPERATIVE

Before discussing our initial efforts in this regard, we feel it is necessary to address a common source of skepticism regarding the possibilities of organic interorganizational collaboration. Specifically, market interactions are often understood in evolutionary terms, according to prevailing conceptions of the "survival of the fittest" dynamic. Within the contemporary culture of contest, moreover, the "survival of the fittest" dynamic is generally understood in competitive terms. Fitness, in other words, is assumed to be a function of self-interested competition.

Yet this competitive view of evolutionary processes says more about the biases of contemporary thought than it does about evolutionary processes. Simply put, "survival of the fittest" is not synonymous with competition. Many evolutionary biologists are now demonstrating that mutualism is an equally powerful, if not more powerful, evolutionary force.[5] Mutualism yielded the emergence of nucleated cells as well as multicellular organisms, which are the basis of all complex life. Mutualism yielded the atmospheric balance of oxygen and carbon dioxide that sustains all forms of complex life today. Mutualism between species, which is abundant in nature, has conferred powerful survival advantages on every species that has taken advantage of this dynamic—from the symbiotic relations between plant roots and nitrogen-fixing microorganisms to the symbiotic relations between humans and the digestion-enhancing microorganisms in our intestinal tracts. Likewise, mutualism within species has conferred survival advantages on all social, or cooperative, species—from ants and bees, to wolves and lions, to primates and humans. And beyond individual species, the complex webs of interdependence that characterize all ecological systems can be understood in terms of complex mutualistic dynamics.

Thus "survival of the fittest" can, to a large extent, be understood as "survival of the mutualist." At a minimum, when we set aside the interpretive biases we have unconsciously internalized from our education and experience within the prevailing culture of contest, we can see that survival of the fittest is clearly not synonymous with competition. Competitive dynamics do exist in nature, to be sure. But the natural order is not exclusively or even primarily characterized by competitive dynamics. Moreover, in our own behavior, as conscious social beings, we have the choice to actualize either our competitive or cooperative potential.

Furthermore, in evolutionary terms, the emergence of increasingly complex organic systems has been characterized, at each evolutionary leap, by the achievement of still higher orders of mutualism and integration—from the emergence of nucleated cells, to the emergence of multicellular organisms, to the emergence of symbiotic relations between dissimilar species, to the emergence of cooperative relations within social species. Likewise, in humanity's collective social evolution, we can see the same dynamic playing out in the emergence of increasingly complex social systems, from the family to the clan to the tribe to the city-state to the nation-state—along with the increasingly complex organizational forms and interactions within and among nation-states today. This succession of advances in social complexity has, in turn, conferred such reproductive and technological advantages on our own species that we have by now completely transformed the conditions of our own existence. Today, we are living in a world of unprecedented social and ecological interdependencies, on a global scale. Yet the cultural codes we have inherited from previous stages in our social evolution—including uncritically held assumptions about human nature and the social order—are proving deeply maladaptive under these new conditions. And the pressure to adapt to this new reality will only continue to mount, in the form of increased social instability and ecological degradation.

Evolution has thus brought us to the threshold of a new social order. We cannot solve the complex social and ecological problems now facing us unless and until we take the next evolutionary step, which entails the development of unprecedented degrees of mutualism and cooperation in our social and economic relations, from the local to the global scale. Thus we can see that organic collaboration is one of the factors that will confer a higher degree of evolutionary fitness. Mutualism, in this contemporary global context, is not an expression of naïve idealism. Rather, it has become an evolutionary imperative at this critical juncture in human history without which the increasingly complex social and economic problems facing humanity cannot be solved.

In this regard, many social entrepreneurs are consciously or unconsciously responding to this evolutionary imperative by engaging in higher-order collaborations in the context of their business models. As they provide products and services where governments and markets have either failed to deliver or not yet reached, many social entrepreneurs are charting new territory by partnering with others in unprecedented ways. Thus social entrepreneurs frequently collaborate with diverse stakeholders, customers, and other partners to better understand complex social and environmental problems, to identify aspects of those problems that can be addressed through market solutions, to develop and finance business models that provide these solutions, and in some cases to nurture entirely new market systems around these models.

LEARNING ABOUT ORGANIC COLLABORATION IN
PRACTICE: THE CASE OF SECONDMUSE

The example of SecondMuse illustrates a conscious, purposeful, and reflective effort to apply the principles of organic collaboration within a social entrepreneurship framework. SecondMuse was formed in 2008 out of the Harmony Equity Group. From the outset, it has sought to redefine the modern corporation as an entity that cocreates shared prosperity and contributes to an ever-advancing civilization. Though this is admittedly a bold goal, a small group of social entrepreneurs motivated by this vision has taken on the challenge. Their initial contribution to this overarching goal is an effort to demonstrate how organic collaboration between diverse private-sector and public-sector partners can address global challenges in impactful ways while advancing the mission of corporations, civil society organizations, and governments.

One of the early initiatives of SecondMuse was Random Hacks of Kindness (RHoK), which has brought together successive waves of volunteers committed to "Hacking for Humanity." Coordinated by SecondMuse since its inception, RHoK is a joint initiative among Google, Yahoo!, Microsoft, NASA, and the World Bank. To date, RHoK has enlisted the skills and energies of global networks of volunteers who develop software solutions in fields as diverse as natural disaster management, biomedical innovations in less-industrialized countries, investment vehicles for marginalized populations, water resource management, and solar power solutions. These volunteer efforts take the form of "hackathons"—intensive weekends of volunteer software development focused on specific social or environmental problems. To date, over 150 RHoK hackathons have been held involving over 10,000 volunteer participants. In June 2012 alone, SecondMuse organized 25 RHoK events in 14 countries—in Africa, Australia, the Caribbean, Europe, the Indian subcontinent, and North America—involving over 900 volunteers working on 132 problem definitions and generating 138 software solutions. Though skeptics initially thought it would be impossible for Google, Yahoo!, Microsoft, NASA, and the World Bank to work together in a sustained collaboration like this, SecondMuse was able to accomplish it in a way that yielded unprecedented outcomes by aligning the event with the business or mission imperatives of each organization, as well as the altruistic motivations of all the individuals involved.

Another SecondMuse initiative is LAUNCH, which brought NASA, USAID, the US State Department, and Nike into a collaborative partnership focused on incubating environmental sustainability initiatives. LAUNCH derives from a recognition that many breakthrough innovations are never successfully brought to scale due to a variety of circumstances that include insufficient funding, management, or marketing skills on the part of innovators. The first event, "LAUNCH: Water," took place in March 2010. It brought together dozens of leading innovators, scientists, entrepreneurs, activists, and government officials in an unconventional, multidisciplinary, and emergent collaborative process that assisted with the launching of some of the world's most impressive water-sustainability innovations. The process began with a global search that identified ten of the most promising new water-sustainability innovations. Innovators were then assisted in a process of developing and honing a presentation of their innovation, which was subsequently given in front of a LAUNCH Council of 60 leading scientists, entrepreneurs, activists, and government officials who, in turn, consulted with each innovator in rotations of small consultative groups. Each group provided each innovator with advice on how to successfully bring the innovation to scale, including technical or business advice as well as contacts and networking opportunities that would assist in the process. Following this event, SecondMuse continued to support an "acceleration" process whereby the input offered during the LAUNCH forum could be translated into rapid and significant progress toward bringing the innovation to scale. Since LAUNCH: Water took place, similar LAUNCH processes have occurred with a focus on Health, Energy, and Waste, respectively. In each of these processes, the whole has clearly been greater than the sum of the parts, as the missions of diverse organizations and the altruistic motivations of diverse individuals have been aligned within emergent collaborative processes.

SecondMuse is involved in numerous other initiatives—all focused on intraorganizational or interorganizational collaborative processes that address significant social or environmental problems—and the company is growing at a rapid pace due to the consistent success of its initiatives. But none of these initiatives were born simply from perceived market opportunities that aligned the generation of revenue with the creation of social good. Rather, they were born from a conceptual framework that offers a radical reconception of a corporation based on a holistic model of human nature, a corresponding conception of social and economic relations, and a commitment to processes of organic collaboration motivated by a desire to contribute to the betterment of the entire social body. From this conceptual framework, a corporation was formed with a mission to learn how to apply the framework in its daily work, in a financially sustainable manner. From this corporation, services and products have been developed that have generated value as social goods. But these services and products are not viewed as ends in themselves. Rather, they are viewed as means to advance a process of learning about the reinvention of the modern corporation. In the process, SecondMuse is challenging inherited economic assumptions that have been uncritically accepted for centuries.

MOVING FORWARD

We stand at a critical juncture in history. There are now seven billion of us on this planet and we are wielding technologies that increase our impact and our interdependence a thousandfold. As a result, we have transformed the conditions of our own existence and are now facing unprecedented social and ecological problems on a global scale. These increasingly complex problems cannot be solved within the frameworks of thought that created them. At the center of these maladaptive frameworks is a self-interested and competitive worldview that fragments our collective intelligence and undermines our collective capacity.

Against this backdrop, social entrepreneurship is one of the many progressive trends that is gathering momentum in the world today. However, social entrepreneurs can and must do more than simply implement new business plans that address specific social or environmental needs with market solutions. They also need to reinvent business itself as a source of shared prosperity within an organically unified and interdependent social body. One aspect of this work involves the development of more effective and sustained modes of collaboration between people and organizations with diverse insights, experience, talents, and capacities. The increasingly complex problems facing humanity today cannot be solved in any other way. The corporation—along with many other human institutions—will ultimately need to be reinvented along lines that promote this kind of organic collaboration. (What Craig Dunn would call a more deliberate disruptive design.)

The initial experience of SecondMuse suggests that such efforts are not only possible, but financially sustainable. Yet there is still much to be learned. The authors therefore invite others to join us as we strive to advance the frontiers of learning in this context.

NOTES

1. There is a rapidly expanding body of empirical evidence supporting this claim. Refer, for instance, Martin Nowak and Roger Highfield, *Super Cooperators: Altruism, Evolution, and Why We Need Each Other to Succeed* (New York: Free Press, 2011); Samuel Bowles and Herbert Gintis, *A Cooperative Species: Human Reciprocity and its Evolution* (Princeton, NJ: Princeton University Press, 2010); Michael Tomasello, *Why We Cooperate* (Boston: Massachusetts Institute of Technology, 2009); *Origins of Human Communication* (Boston: Massachusetts Institute of Technology, 2008); Jeremy Rifkin, *The Empathic Civilization: The Race to Global Consciousness in a World in Crisis* (New York: Penguin Books, 2009); Frans de Waal, *The Age of Empathy: Nature's Lessons for a Kinder Society* (New York: Three Rivers Press, 2009); Robert Axelrod, *The Evolution of Cooperation*, revised edition (New York: Basic Books, 2006); Nigel Barber, *Kindness in a Cruel World: The Evolution of Altruism* (Amherst, NY: Prometheus Books, 2004); Elliott Sober and David Sloan Wilson, *Unto Others: The Evolution of Psychology and Unselfish Behavior* (Harvard University Press, 2003); Kristen Monroe, *The Heart of Altruism: Perceptions of a Common Humanity* (Princeton, NJ: Princeton University Press, 1998); Matt Ridley, *The Origins of Virtue: Human Instincts and the Evolution of Cooperation* (New York: Penguin Books, 1998); Robert Wright, *The Moral Animal: Why We Are the Way We Are: The New Science of Evolutionary Psychology* (New York: Vintage Books, 1995).
2. Michael Karlberg, *Beyond the Culture of Contest: From Adversarialism to Mutualism in an Age of Interdependence* (Oxford: George Ronald, 2004).
3. Refer, e.g., Alfie Kuhn, *No Contest: The Case against Competition: Why We All Lose in Our Race to Win* (New York: Houghton Mifflin Company, 1992); and *Punished by Rewards* (New York: Houghton Mifflin Company, 1999).
4. Michael Karlberg, "Reframing Public Discourse for Peace and Justice," in Kristina Korostelina (ed.), *Forming a Culture of Peace: Reframing Narratives of Intergroup Relations, Equity, and Justice* (Palgrave Macmillan, 2012), pp. 15–42.
5. Refer, e.g., Boris Mikhaylovich Kozo-Polyansky, Lynn Margulis, Victor Fet, and Peter Raven, *Symbiogenesis: A New Principle of Evolution.* (Harvard University Press, 2010); and Lynn Margulis, *Symbiotic Planet: A New Look at Evolution* (Amherst, MA: Basic Books, 1998).

Chapter 12

BUILDING GREEN ECONOMY THINKING

Greg Wendt
Green Economy Think Tank

AS A PRIVATE WEALTH ADVISOR, community activist, and green economy advocate, I am committed to shifting the global economy to a partnership between people and nature dedicated to creating a thriving civilization, which supports health and happiness. By the time I found myself at a desk in Smith Barney in 1991 on the fifty-second floor of an office tower in Downtown LA, I had already become a passionate environmentalist— ironically catalyzed through an international association of economics students. Through my participation at the UCLA chapter of AIESEC, an international student organization in five hundred universities, I learned the term "sustainable development," defined as "development that meets the needs of the present without compromising the ability of future generations to meet their own needs."

Shortly after working at Smith Barney, I learned about "socially responsible investing" (SRI), which I quickly decided would become my career. Today, SRI is known by a range of terms such as "sustainable and responsible investing," "ethical investing," "impact investing," "green investing," and so on, all referring to the process of incorporating environmental, governance, and social factors in the context of a rigorous investment discipline.

In 2002, after the Internet boom and bust, after a second, more expensive adventure into Iraq by the US military, and the accelerating pace of rapacious consumption of the planet's resources by ever-increasing economic activity, I came to the conclusion that the prevailing economic operating system was no longer working for all of humanity. The global "casino" of financial markets had to a great extent lost touch with the quality of life in local communities, and the quality of life of the very biosphere within which our economy functions.

What seemed clear was the global financial system had gone out of control.

As John Fullerton, founder of The Capital Institute, made clear on their website (www.capitalinstitute.org), "Exponential growth of the macro economy is in conflict with the physical limitations of a finite planet. The incompatibility of the current economic and financial paradigm, one that operates without ecosystem limits, has caused immeasurable social and environmental damage and threatens the future health and well-being of the planet."

It is also clear that if this observation were indeed true, it was also true that the "economic system is an integral part of the natural biosphere within which it sits. Our financial and economic systems, while continuing to provide for society's needs, must evolve to work in concert with the planet's systems. Although challenging, such a transformation is possible through innovative thinking, the pioneering of new designs and solutions, and bold and decisive action." This recognition underscores the notion that if we transform the way money is we can simultaneously address issues such as the needs of communities, quality of life, human justice, food quality, education, infrastructure, energy security, and soil fertility.

Yet the question remains, how and where does this transformation need to happen?

Even if the responsible investment movement were successful in transforming the operations of every major publicly traded company on the planet to sustainability, we would still need a deeper systemic change. I recognized that something fundamental needed to shift in the way we do business in every single community.

Around that time, I met Judy Wicks at the fall 2002 Social Venture Network conference. Judy is a woman whose approach to business has had a huge influence on my worldview. She is an entrepreneur who charismatically ran a restaurant in Philadelphia called White Dog Café. She said she ran the cafe with the driving intention to "maximize relationships over maximizing profits."

Judy and her network of friends recognized their businesses were actually a tapestry of relationships, a network, and they founded the Sustainable Business Network of Philadelphia (SBN). SBN became the founding chapter of an organization called Business Alliance for Local Living Economies (BALLE). Today, BALLE is the fastest growing green and socially responsible business movement in the country with networks in over 80 cities and 23,000 business members nationwide.

In order for an economic transaction to succeed, it must be built on the collaboration and trust between people in the economy. From trust, we build the value dynamics in quality exchange and the better the quality of exchange we can build, the better outcomes we have within our business transactions.

BRING IT HOME

It became clear to me that by simply incorporating the quality of relationships back into the economy we have the potential to transmute our current economy of waste into an economy of thriving abundance, conservation, and renewal for the well-being of all life on the planet. Back home, I realized that there was an opportunity to build community and connections between the owners and decision-makers of socially and environmentally-conscious businesses by simply providing them a time and place for connecting, sharing, deal-making and networking. In April 2006 I led a group of local leaders to invite green business owners to launch LA's BALLE network, with a monthly event. We have held events every month since our inception with 25–250 attendees, and the subscriber list for our newsletters has grown to over 4,500 business owners, investors, consultants, professionals, all who are focused on building a green economy. We promote and coproduce events with nearly every other social enterprise and green economy group in the region.

In 2008, our group realized that another leg of the green economy needed to be built beyond the community of businesses—we needed better coordination and connection among all the agents in the region's economy, which could bring about better results, and provide more fertile soil to support greener business practices and green entrepreneurship. Every year there are well-attended annual conferences on green business, sustainable professional practices, renewable energy, and energy efficiency, all of them hosted with the vision of greening Los Angeles and building a green economy for the region. Many of the participants in all of these events are leading experts in their fields, who keynote at conferences, lead their organization's sustainability efforts, yet they don't all meet together to discuss collaboration. I recognized that there was a fundamental missing link while connecting the dots between all of the activities in the LA region. Surprisingly no one had yet organized an action-oriented event dedicated solely to convene leaders to build a shared vision and prioritize the green economy where we all live.

The synergy and connectivity among participants in a multisector collaborative event like this further catalyzes the network of green economy participants into better solutions and more effective partnerships. We saw the promise and power of crowd intelligence applied in economics of place. By moving beyond the traditional panel and speaker model we created working conversations focused on regional solutions, bringing ideas into action through an innovative collective intelligence process throughout the event to filter the best ideas with the most support into a shared vision.

IT DOESN'T ALWAYS WORK THE WAY IT'S PLANNED

In 2008 I approached a major university extension to produce our first conference, with the vision that we'd hold a two-day event with 200–250 leaders participating from the LA region.

Our planning committee held community-building luncheons with key leaders from LA's environmental groups, green business owners, and civic representatives to create the invitation list and define the scope and vision of the event. After six months of planning, coordination, and meetings, we had a major setback—the university decided to pull out and leave the project in our hands. After some soul searching, gnashing of teeth, and regrouping, our team decided to move forward with the event. We remained committed to producing an event on the same date, yet scaled it back to a half-day conference, which would build a better framework to lead up to a bigger event in the future.

Our summer 2009 half-day Green Economy Think Tank Day event created a multistakeholder vision for a LA's Green Economy, which identified opportunities, barriers, and mechanisms to further our individual and collective goals. The success of this conference was our first step in building a network of key relationships and connecting existing efforts for shared success.

FINDING NEW PARTNERS AND BUILDING ON THE FOUNDATION

After the initial conference, it was clear that our original volunteer team did not have the capacity to create another event. Fortunately, in early 2010, the City of Santa Monica Sustainability Department approached us and offered to coproduce a larger conference with our team. This partnership with the city was a major milestone for our organization—our success was found again in matching a small team of volunteer community organizers in partnership with a major institution for the broader community. In August 2010, we convened over 120 leaders from the LA region to an invitation-only leadership event with content based on the findings and recommendations from our first conference. Facilitated breakout groups were led by key experts, collectively designed to create action-oriented discussions on six pertinent topics:

- capital and collaboration for green economy initiatives;
- financing solar installations;
- buying local campaigns;
- media and green economy;
- sustainability in all levels of education; and
- harmonizing the various green business certification efforts throughout the region.

A number of the initiatives outlined in the conference are growing, and partnerships forged at the event continue to implement the vision and efforts identified in the conference.

REPLICATING OUR SUCCESS

In the fall of 2010, the San Francisco Department of Environment learned of our efforts and decided to create a Bay Area version of our Green Economy Think Tank Day with our team. They wanted to inform the new San Francisco mayor about actions and guidelines to support job creation and industry in alignment with the city's climate action plan. The event was built on the model of a partnership between key collaborating organizations and was titled "San Francisco Green Economic Forum—Jobs and Opportunity in a Changing Climate." Our partners were the San Francisco Department of the Environment, Office of Economic and Workforce Development, job training providers, other government agencies, and leading businesses to discuss the green job landscape in San Francisco. There were discussions of implementation of San Francisco's multistakeholder climate action plan and a report back from five community advisory panels. The mayor and the Department of the Environment are still working to implement the recommendations from our conference.

BUILDING A NETWORK IN CITIES ACROSS THE COUNTRY

We continue to sustain our efforts through our partnership model by strengthening relationships with key partners in every city where we now have volunteers. In addition to our conferences and events in Los Angeles and San Francisco we have teams building on the ground in New Orleans, New York, Chicago, Washington DC, Portland, and Fresno, CA. In the Los Angeles region, Green Economy Think Tank and our partners are incubating programs based on our 2010 conference in neighbor-to-neighbor lending, complimentary currency, membership programs, partnerships with industry groups, online initiatives, all to serve the growing community of the tens of thousands of people leading the green economy movement.

Although both Green Business Networking and Green Economy Think Tank continue to be volunteer run, we are in the process of raising the necessary funds to create a full-time staff. Further, the partnerships, actions, and recommendations from our conferences and the communities they convened have inspired my current project called California Innovation Fund (CIF). CIF aims to develop public benefit economic development at the intersection of crowdfunding, green economy, community collective intelligence, economic development, and venture capital and public/private partnerships. In addition to the sustenance that the nonprofit efforts create, my partners and I envision that our for-profit businesses will partner with the work of Green Economy Think Tank. Our mission is to continue to develop solutions and inspire leaders to harness the power of relationships and collective intelligence for a better economy for future generations in cities across the country and the world.

Part 3

DEFINING THE SOCIAL EDGE: EDUCATION AND SOCIAL WELL-BEING

Liberty cannot be preserved without a general knowledge among the people. The preservation of the means of knowledge among the lowest ranks is of more importance to the public than all the property of all the rich men in the country.

—John Adams, *Dissertation on the Canon and the Federal Law* (1765)

OUR FUTURE IS NOT PREDICATED ON ECONOMIC forecasts or the latest style trends or the next remake of a remake in Hollywood. It is, however, inseparable from the level of education we are providing our young people and the opportunities that emerge from how they are taught. In an era of cutbacks, growing classrooms, and reduced time actually spent in learning, how we educate our young people today will have a direct reflection on how our society thrives or declines in the future. This is an investment we cannot afford to miss, and yet it is now the first and deepest cut we see being made across the board.

In the United States, the issue of students dropping out of high school is not only alarming, it is a life sentence to those we allow to slip away from the system. In 2012, according to the National Center for Educational Statistics, only seven out of ten ninth graders will be around to get their high-school diplomas. And the racial gap is not really reflected in these numbers. Approximately 80 percent of all white and Asian students graduate from high school. In contrast, only 55 percent of blacks and Hispanics complete their high-school education. Those numbers translate directly into opportunities for those who move forward with their education and opportunities that are not even available to those who do not.

When Dorothy Stoneman founded YouthBuild there was a local need in Harlem that she recognized had to be met. The dropout rate was increasing and generations of opportunities were not just being lost, they weren't even options on the table. Her program was a simple idea, to put these kids who had fallen through the seams of our educational system to work, restoring the deteriorating homes in the area. The deal they made with Dorothy was they spent six months learning how to put up walls, sheet rock, paint rooms, and so on, and six months were spent working toward getting a high-school GED. While YouthBuild uses education as its driver, Stoneman believes it is really an antipoverty program. Providing opportunity, through education, where it didn't exist before.

Today, there are over 250 YouthBuild programs operating around the United States with more launching in Europe. The model and program work. The students work. And suddenly, where there was no future, opportunities emerge. It's really not so surprising what dedication, perseverance, and love can accomplish, but we always seem to be unprepared for the results that come when they are employed. When we design programs that create new options for people, a whole new realm of possibilities show up that never seemed to be there before. It's not magic, unless, of course, magic is being transformed by the unexpected. That's what Dorothy Stoneman has been able to conjure, transforming the lives of children from whom we expected the worst.

Gary Kosman showed up in my office at Volunteers of America, Los Angeles, just as I was launching our Social Entrepreneur Incubator. He was bright, eager, and had begun an operation providing tutors connection and resources that had previously been unavailable to them. If tutors were being employed to raise the abilities of our students, it would make sense that we make sure these tutors had a way of handling situations for which they might not be prepared. Gary connected them to each other, to experts, and to the resources they required to get their job done to improve the educational experience of students. Today, America Learns has broadened its program to providing web-based services to volunteer and national service program leaders so they can track, report, and evaluate what's happening with their folks delivering services in the field. And they are succeeding because of the same commitment to helping others learn that was evident in my office over a decade ago.

Our social landscape spreads out far and wide; what and how we learn to view the opportunities and options spread out along that landscape depends on the service of those willing to share what they know. We don't come into this world with all the knowledge we need: an understanding of history, an ability to read and write, a sense of how the material world operates physically, what infects it, what limits it. Without those dedicated to sharing what they know and helping us traverse through that landscape, we can become subjugated by those who wish to exploit it. A society dedicated to education is one that is willing to question "how things have always been done" to find new solutions to make that landscape flourish for everyone living on it.

Chapter 13

BUILDING FUNDAMENTAL PRINCIPLES

Dorothy Stoneman
Youth Build

WHEN I STARTED THE YOUTH ACTION PROGRAM, the precursor of YouthBuild, in East Harlem in 1978, the term "social entrepreneur" did not exist, nor was I aware of any principles, technical assistance, business planning consulting firms, or social investors focused on "scaling social innovations." Fortunately, foundations were attuned to finding people with good ideas for solving social problems, and social activism was understood as a good. The Charles Stewart Mott Foundation and the Ford Foundation discovered my work and supported it for decades.

I was building on my experience in the Civil Rights Movement as well as my experience as an organizer, teacher, and administrator of programs funded through the Office of Economic Opportunity (OEO) in the short-lived antipoverty program of the 1960s. I had been living and working in Harlem and East Harlem since 1964, when I had moved from Harvard to Harlem and joined the Civil Rights Movement through the grassroots storefront Harlem Action Group on 8th Avenue and 137th Street.

By 1974 I had decided that it was my moral obligation to do everything in my power to build a constituency that could collectively take power to decisively change the United States to eliminate poverty and to distribute opportunity and responsibility to all citizens in a way that would allow every child born to fulfill his or her highest aspirations and contribute to the well-being of humanity. I had started a naïve but wonderful New Action Party for a Human Society, organized 70 friends, and written a 50-year plan for transforming America.

By 1978 we had chosen five key areas in which decisive change was needed, and selected one of these—creating opportunities for low-income youth—as our central action program through which we would demonstrate that we had the wisdom and skill to build something so good that it would give us the credibility to run for office and take sufficient power to spread our principles of shared opportunity and responsibility to the entire society.

The receipt of federal funds through a competitive grant process to implement the Youth Action Program in 1978 forced me to turn my attention from building a new political party to implementing the central action program on the ground. The party dissolved, because clearly we couldn't use federal funds to build a political party, but the fundamental goals of building a movement for maximum impact did not.

Throughout the following 34 years, it has been my role to balance the complex process of building an expanding grassroots constituency committed to eliminating poverty, with the equally complex process of obtaining an ever-expanding pool of resources from the federal government, and other private and public sources, to do this. Since I believed it was a public responsibility to build effective systems of opportunity for all, obtaining public funds was a core part of our strategy, and engaging young people in advocating for those funds and policies was part of the leadership development process.

Of course it had to start with demonstrating and codifying for replication a highly successful approach to engaging the most disadvantaged young people in rebuilding their own communities and their own lives while learning to become leaders willing to take long-term responsibility for their communities. This effort was named YouthBuild in 1988, 10 years after it had been launched, and just before we took it national. The next 24 years required my attention to make sure that this highly successful program was replicated with fidelity to the philosophy and program design. I needed to make sure that the public-private partnership was workable and robust, and that sufficient bipartisan political support was built to sustain its federal funding.

Today, our YouthBuild graduates are maturing into sophisticated and responsible change agents, who I encourage to organize to produce a commitment to end poverty in the United States. Furthermore, since we are now working internationally, a larger goal of diminishing poverty worldwide is in our sights.

What we have achieved concretely in the first 34 years can be summarized this way:

- 120,000 low-income YouthBuild students have produced 22,000 units of affordable housing for homeless and low-income people in their communities, while working toward their own high-school diploma or GED, learning job skills, and preparing for college, careers, and community leadership.
- A total of 273 communities have generated local leadership sufficient to establish and sustain YouthBuild programs through their own initiative in urban and rural communities in 45 states within the United States, using the $1.3 billion of federal dollars made available to them through our advocacy for the YouthBuild program that was first authorized in federal law in 1992. At the same time, due to the unpredictability of federal investment, another 100 YouthBuild programs have opened and then had to close for lack of funds. This is the tragic underside of the persistent lack of political will in the United States to end poverty.
- The leadership of these programs has come together in a cohesive national network.
- An uncounted but substantial number of graduates have become effective local leaders and all graduates have created a powerful and immeasurable ripple effect by helping other people in their families and neighborhoods.

- Because we have been so successful in the United States, 16 other countries have brought the principles of YouthBuild to their shores and already created 56 local programs, while laying the groundwork for scaling up with their own government funds. This has occurred in South Africa, Mexico, Israel, Haiti, Brazil, and many other countries.

The fundamental principles inherent in our beginnings, and in our success to date, are outlined here.

FUNDAMENTAL PRINCIPLES

We seek to join with others to help build a movement toward a more just society in which respect, love, responsibility, and cooperation are the dominant unifying values, and sufficient opportunities are available for all people in all communities to fulfill their own potential and contribute to the well-being of others.

PHILOSOPHY

The intelligence and positive energy of young people need to be liberated and enlisted in solving the problems facing our society. Young people in low-income communities want to rebuild their neighborhoods and lives, and will do so if given the opportunity. The desire to serve, to do meaningful work that is of value to other people, is universal. Community-based organizations need the resources to solve local problems and to mobilize local people, including neighborhood youth. Leadership development is a central element of effective community and youth development.

CORE UNDERLYING CONVICTIONS

Every human life is sacred, full of potential, and worthy of love.

Human beings have the potential to create a good society in which mutual respect and a reasonably just distribution of resources and opportunities are the dominant realities. Achieving such a society is the central challenge that faces us as a species.

Individuals are decisively influenced by the communities in which they are raised and in which they live. Communities that have a rich set of opportunities, caring relationships, high expectations, and that are organized to meet the needs of their members and the children within them are the foundation of a healthy society.

Every community needs ethical, caring, committed leaders who have the best interests of the community members at heart and are skilled in bringing people together to set goals, implement ideas, and solve problems. Leadership development is at the heart of community development.

Young people are capable of playing a leadership role and if encouraged to do so will bring enormous energy, creativity, and imagination to the work. Existing leaders should bring young leaders to the table.

SOME LESSONS LEARNED

If I were giving advice to individual aspiring social entrepreneurs, I would share with them the following list of personal lessons I have learned about what it takes to achieve any level of impact in the spheres of community development, movement-building, and poverty alleviation.

1. *Decision*: It matters what you decide to do. Nothing big ever happens unless you decide to make it happen.
2. *Persistence*: Nothing important ever happens if you give up.
3. *Support*: Friends, family, colleagues, and all forms of communities of support matter—you can't build a positive force alone. You may be able to write a paper or a convincing proposal alone, but you can't build a movement for social change alone.
4. *Partners*: Both work partners and lifetime personal partners who support your vision make a world of difference. For example, my husband, John Bell, has been key to my persistence and well-being, and as a VP at YouthBuild USA has contributed to all of our victories.
5. *Awareness*: We live in a society where racism, classism, sexism, heterosexism, ageism, and adultism suffuse our lives and experiences. Everyone's experiences and worldviews are influenced profoundly by these forces. We have to work to understand the impact of them. We must step outside the limits of our own experience to learn about

the world from many points of view. The best learning experience is to embed yourself in a community totally different from your own for at least a year, or many years, or several different communities, long enough to internalize a new viewpoint, and realize how limited your previous viewpoint was.

6. *Accountability*: Anyone aiming to produce something that benefits any community of people needs to set up structures that make them directly accountable to that community. And of course, once we get government and philanthropic dollars we need to be accountable to produce what we promise.

7. *Integrity and reliability*: Never do anything you would have to lie about and always do what you say you're going to do. This is what builds your reputation and the trust of other people. Without their trust, nothing gets done. Maintain integrity down to the details, even when nobody is looking: for example, when the taxi driver, who seems to have been trained by customers to give them blank receipts so they can pad them for their reimbursement, gives you a blank receipt, fill it out perfectly accurately.

8. *Kindness and respect*: To build an organization that holds together, where people care about each other and the mission, and are empowered to give their fullest and best, they need to be treated with kindness and respect at all times, even when you have to fire someone for some good reason. Respect includes clarity about what they can expect from the organization and rapid resolution of issues affecting them. It's also important never to talk negative about people behind their back. They will always hear it. It will always create pain and drama and be disruptive to what you are trying to do. Deliberately pass along the positive feedback; avoid and oppose any negative gossip.

9. *Diversity*: If you're building an organization, pay attention to getting different perspectives to the table at every level of the organization and in sufficient numbers to make sure that you have true representation. You will get better decisions and create a healthier community that counteracts the distorted dominant views of the larger society.

10. *Champions*: Find people with greater power than you in a variety of settings who will act as champions of your initiatives. In YouthBuild's case Senator John Kerry and Mott Foundation president Bill White have been the two most important champions over the longest period of time. You need as many champions as you can muster.

11. *Personal healing*: We all come to the work with emotional weaknesses and behavior patterns that are based in early experiences and are counterproductive. We need a system for dumping painful emotion and emerging from limiting and self-destructive ideas and patterns of behavior. There are many approaches worth trying until you find what works best for you.

12. *Mentors*: Pick the smartest, most generous people you admire the most and try to learn from them and ask them to help you. They will be honored.

13. *Humility*: Be aware how little you actually know. Listening to other people is key. Cool out your ego. It's not about you. You're a servant of the people, a servant of God if you wish, but don't let it become about you. It's easy for ego to sneak in. Try to resist.

14. *Defy conventional wisdom*: Don't believe what conventional wisdom says about what's possible or necessary. Use your own best judgment about what would create an optimal situation and what would counteract the injustices we are accustomed to. When I started the first YouthBuild program in 1978 the officials said, "Don't bother. It won't work. Those youth can't build a building. They're high school dropouts. They have no discipline, no skill, no perseverance. Forget it."

15. *Resist materialistic pressures*: When I first got funding for the Youth Action Program in 1978, a young man named Tony Minor, who was 14 at the time, said, "Oh, I get it. A bunch of people are going to get salaries—they'll get rich off our poverty—and we're going to stay poor. That's how these things work." I told him I wouldn't let that happen. Recently, when I read the Chronicle of Philanthropy report that a number of CEOs of nonprofits are paying themselves $500,000, I found it disturbing. The unofficial rule I have followed at YouthBuild USA is that the top salary is no more than five times the

lowest salary. When I started the Youth Action Program in 1978 we made all the salaries equal. Surprisingly, the federal agency that gave us our first grant told me we couldn't do that: the director had to be paid more. My board later told me the same thing in 1990. Salary inequality is deeply embedded in our culture. Try to minimize it.

16. *Manage your disappointment in the gap between your vision and the reality you have created:* This is the sad part. Over time, nobody achieves their full vision. Our heroes, Martin Luther King, Nelson Mandela, Mahatma Ghandi, and everyone else you admire changed the world and inspired millions, but were surely deeply disappointed in the gap between what they tried to do and what they were able to do. Right now Bill Gates is managing his disappointment in not having already transformed the public school system. The day it dawned on me that all these heroes share that disappointment, I decided to start enjoying what I had actually created instead of being disappointed or even ashamed for having failed to create what I had envisioned.

I believe what my mother always said: "The wheels of justice grind slow, but exceedingly fine." And what Martin Luther King said: "The arc of time bends toward justice." Someday, somehow, humanity will create a just society filled with opportunity, love, and responsibility for all, coupled with respect for nature and a commitment to preserve the planet.

If we fail to do that, we could so damage our planet that it might destroy our own species along with the many others that have already been lost. I hope we are too smart to do that. But it will take all hands on deck to create the rational and good society that we can envision. Survival of the fittest in the current era will require cooperation among those most fit to create a cooperative caring society in harmony with mother earth.

Chapter 14

RAISING THE LEARNING CURVE

Gary Kosman
America Learns

I WAS RAISED IN WHAT MANY WOULD consider to be an at-risk family structure: My parents divorced when I was six months old; my mom and I lived in my grandparents' home for eight years; and, due to financial constraints, my mom and I spent about a year living with a person she was dating. Yet, despite these structural differences from traditional family life, my parents and grandparents kept a laser focus on me and my education; and during elementary school, if it wasn't for two key tutors who my mom made sure I had, I'm not sure I would have made it through socially or academically.

Fast forward to my sophomore year of college: I just returned to campus from an internship at the US Department of Education, where there was a ton of buzz around President Clinton's "America Reads Challenge"—an effort to engage thousands of college students as reading tutors in schools and after-school programs. I started tutoring immediately, but found that my fellow tutors and I were constantly failing the students who we were trying to serve.

We knew how to read; but, we didn't have the skills to help children develop those skills. And the organization where we served, though good-intentioned, lacked the capacity to properly train and support its tutors. The organization also lacked the capacity to track what was really going on between the tutors and students, including whether the students were even benefitting from the service. The desire was there; the capacity wasn't. The idea of "well, at least we have volunteers" was good enough.

But it wasn't good enough for the children. As I got to know the students, I found that many of them were labeled "at risk" for the same reasons I could have been labeled that way when I was their age: their parents split, their grandparents were helping to raise them, money was scarce, and their parents were sometimes kicked out of the homes where they were living. I started researching other volunteer-driven tutoring initiatives across the country and found that the scenario I ran into was being replicated nationwide: really good-intentioned organizations were created to help their communities' struggling students because schools didn't have funding to hire highly qualified educators or services to reach these students. These good-intentioned organizations decided they'd address the problem by recruiting good-intentioned volunteers, but the organizations often lacked the capacity to support and monitor the tutors. Promises being made to these children and their families were not being kept.

While my family had the resources to send me to a school with amazing tutors and to hire a terrific after-school tutor for me, that isn't the case for most of the children who are targeted by volunteer-driven tutoring initiatives. Having been raised by a mother who taught me to act on the injustices I see in the world, I reached a point where I could either fight against the nation's volunteer establishment in educational settings, or do whatever it took to help ensure that volunteer tutors serving children always delivered on the promises being made to those kids and their families. Believing that the first option wasn't achievable at the time, I chose the latter.

The core philosophies behind the services we provide were developed during several independent studies I undertook while in college. I was fortunate to have incredible professors who mentored me as I studied how teachers learn, and then worked to apply those insights to the volunteer tutoring field. As I did more research, I created a pilot program with a professor that worked to track and support my fellow college students who were volunteering as tutors in the community. That pilot worked out fairly well; but, it required far too much manpower to maintain and scale. I spent the next several years working three jobs and storyboarding a web service that would automate that manpower. To make sure I was on the right track, I shared and improved those storyboards during hundreds of meetings with volunteers, tutors, teachers, parent advocates, e-learning experts, and others.

Those storyboards, and a short-term failure to secure funding to hire a web developer to turn those storyboards into a functional service, eventually led me to teach myself enough HTML to build a working prototype of the system. I then used the results of that pilot to secure seed funding from Echoing Green and really get the company going.

None of this was easy. There were three personal obstacles that stood in the way of getting America Learns going: staying healthy, learning to trust others with my dream, and learning how to sell.

STAYING HEALTHY

I realized that, in its early years, this company would only continue to exist if I continued to exist. Eventually, this thinking led to practices such as rarely working on weekends and giving all of our employees two afternoons off each week so they can pursue their own self-care practices. America Learns runs on a belief that the only way our customers can come first is if our team members' physical and emotional well-being comes first.

LEARNING TO TRUST OTHERS WITH MY DREAM

For various reasons nearly all of the web engineers who I've worked with to build and manage our web services work one thousand or more miles from our offices in Los Angeles. The process of learning to build trusting relationships with people I didn't interact with physically, but who literally determined the short-term success or failure of the company each day, was extremely challenging. I took each bug as a personal attack waged by my engineers on me. Entrepreneurial insanity. While we continued to innovate and serve our clients well, relations between me and my engineers were often sour, leading to sleepless nights, ridiculous amounts of stress, and high turnover.

But then I met Selah, a leadership and management training program run by the Rockwood Leadership Institute and Bend the Arc. The program taught me how to lead from a distance, how to watch and respond to my emotions when unexpected problems occur, how to build trust with those one doesn't interact with in the physical realm, and how to have difficult-yet-calm conversations with colleagues and others. I've used these skills to build a strong, stable team of incredible engineers and other team members who are spread across the United States and around the world.

LEARNING HOW TO SELL AND LEARNING TO TRAIN OUR SALES FORCE

Our business requires an exceptionally strong sales force; yet, when I started the company, I had no experience with selling any type of services (let alone training others to do so).

After several years of mediocre results with email blasts and cold calls, I was introduced to Thomas Freese's book *The Secrets of Question Based Selling*.[1] The book has completely transformed our company, helping us achieve our social mission on a far larger scale by shortening our average sales cycle from 18 months to 3.

Here are three types of skills we now employ daily:

- *We've killed the canned demonstrations of our service.* Now, each demonstration is preceded by up to 40 minutes of questions and conversation in which we become short-term consultants for the organization. The rest of the demonstration shows exactly how our service could be used by the prospect.
- *We help the prospect uncover "latent needs."* For example, in the AmeriCorps community, most program leaders have it drilled into their heads that they need to collect and report accurate "performance measurement data," and so a number of companies have popped up to help them do that and program leaders spend a tremendous amount

of time collecting that data throughout the year. But performance measurement data collection doesn't yield outcomes. It's our job to ask our prospects about the most important data they need to collect that they think they'll never need to report to their funders. Most program leaders are taken aback by this question because they rarely have time to even think about collecting data that won't be reported. As our service was designed to help leaders collect and use whatever they need, helping program leaders think about a reality in which they can have it all, and then using the demonstration process described earlier to show them exactly "what it all" looks like is huge.

- *We strive to be impartial consultants.* To me, it's far more important that any potential client of ours find the best solution for them, than to sign a contract with us. If, after our introductory questions we feel that our service isn't the best one for the prospect, we'll recommend the services of other companies. We also recommend the services of competitors even when our service is appropriate, because we want to make sure the prospect is investing in what's best for them. On occasion, even after we point out that our service doesn't do everything a prospect needs in comparison to another service, the prospect still chooses to partner with us simply because he or she appreciated our honesty and our approach of partnering with, rather than selling to our clients.

CULTURAL OBSTACLES

During our early days, a number of clients stopped using our services in less than a year. After conducting a number of interviews with clients (both those who had success with us and those who did not), I learned that there were significant differences between our successful and our frustrated clients.

Our successful clients had employees who formally assessed the capacity of their organizations to use and manage our services well *before* a contract was signed. Those clients also developed a concrete plan to introduce and implement our services in a way that blended with their organizations' existing cultures around collecting data, using data, and supporting their people on the ground.

Most organizations we serve do not have employees who are expert change management consultants, so we've taken it upon ourselves to provide these services to our prospects and customers. Now, before we sign a contract with an organization, we walk that organization's team through an exercise that assesses their capacity to use our services well. Once a contract is signed, we create a formal "culture integration" plan to ensure that there's rapid buy-in for our services. These steps have not only led to 100 percent or near-100 percent customer retention from year to year; they've also led to faster sales cycles and far fewer customer support requests.

Since America Learns launched, our mission and reach has changed significantly. While we started out focused solely on volunteer-driven tutoring organizations, we've learned that the services we built solved a much larger problem in organizations within and outside of the nonprofit and social change communities. Just about every organization needs to collect and use data. The problem comes when just one person (or a small team of people) needs to do all of that work alone. We solve that problem for school districts, nonprofits of all shapes and sizes, NGOs, government entities, medical schools, and others.

As our client base has expanded and grown in size, we created three divisions of our company: one that serves the tutoring and youth development community; one that serves other nonprofit and social justice organizations; and one that serves government and business. Customers that fall into the first two divisions pay a reduced annual license fee to use our services, while other organizations pay higher fees. Portions of those higher fees are funneled into our first two divisions to keep our services affordable. America Learns has been profitable since 2005.

NOTE

1. Thomas Freese, *The Secrets of Question Based Selling*, first edition (Sourcebooks, Inc., 2000).

Part 4

DELIBERATELY DISRUPTIVE TECHNOLOGY

Here's to the crazy ones, the misfits, the rebels, the troublemakers, the round pegs in the square holes…the ones who see things differently—they're not fond of rules…You can quote them, disagree with them, glorify or vilify them, but the only thing you can't do is ignore them because they change things…they push the human race forward, and while some may see them as the crazy ones, we see genius, because the ones who are crazy enough to think that they can change the world, are the ones who do.

—Steve Jobs

INNOVATIVE TECHNOLOGIES HAVE BEEN at the forefront of our economy for decades. Few advances in other fields produce as great a return or have created more gazillionaires than our technological innovators have. There was once an article that delineated the amount of money the great basketball player Michael Jordan was making at the height of his career—breaking it down by the month, week, hour, minute, and second. Each segmentation, in turn, seemed like an astronomical sum, until the final line of the article that stated that Jordan would have to make his total income every year for about 180 years to equal what Bill Gates made in one.

The gold created in technology valleys from Silicon to Boston to Bangalore has dwarfed traditional industries and established a generation of young and wealthy like few eras in history. Developing technologies that solve pressing social problems and whose deliberate disruptive design makes them available to everyone who needs them is often a hard sell when the lure of more and more awaits the technological wizard who can envision the next "new and now" (the root words of innovation) advance.

The truth is there are many social entrepreneurs exploring how technology might shift our old ways of doing business. And all of them are not software driven. Two prominent examples are represented here, MacArthur Genius Grant award winner Jim Fruchterman, CEO of Benetech, and Bart Weetjens, who launched Apopo, and whose Vapor Detection Technology revolutionized landmine detection and their elimination by training Africa's Giant Rats, HeroRats as they are known, to safely sniff out the bombs so that they can be removed, without ever harming a single rat hair.

These two social entrepreneurs have simply ignored the hurdles most technology companies encounter by creating innovative solutions by seeing the landscape before them and figuring out what's missing and then coming up with a deliberate disruptive design to fill the void. This is not the only approach to creating technological solutions that impact the world in which we operate. One might also decide to take a look at that same landscape to see what could be there but which is not missing at all. What might the next telephone, television, personal computer, Ipod, or Ipad technology be? No one ever knew these technologies were missing from the environment and yet now many couldn't live without them.

The real challenge for technology and social entrepreneurship is three-fold: (1) to figure out ways of getting it into the hands of the poorest of the poor, (2) activating those factors that influence cultural and personal adoption of the technology, and (3) creating the partnerships necessary to distribute the technology into its intended market. From both Benetech and Apopo, we have technology that goes straight to those who need it. None of it will ever make the founders of these companies rich like Bill Gates, or even Michael Jordan, but neither of them are engaged in this work to realize those results. The deliberate disruptions they are designing create a world in which technology serves those who need it most, not one where the latest technological distraction device isolates us further from the world in which we all want to live healthy and secure lives.

Chapter 15

TECHNOLOGY SERVING HUMANITY

Jim Fruchterman
Benetech

BENETECH IS SILICON VALLEY'S NONPROFIT software company. Our team builds products to meet the needs of the social sector, products that the for-profit world would fail to build because they would be insufficiently profitable. In most cases, the basic technology already exists and can be easily adapted for social good. And, once built, it's easy to scale up technology to help huge numbers of people inexpensively. Benetech focuses our efforts in three specific areas where we think we can make a big difference with software: human rights, the environment, and education.

I was motivated to start Benetech because an optical character recognition technology I had helped invent at a for-profit company could help people with disabilities—specifically people who were blind or visually impaired. However, it wasn't a big enough market, so our investors tabled the project. Benetech was born as a nonprofit spin-out of that for-profit company.

Over more than 20 years, we've grown from our first product, a reading machine for the blind, to multiple products. Over time, we've gotten more ambitious and we now hope to launch a major new product each year. As we've grown, we've learned what works for us and have codified two frameworks that guide our team. Benetech's New Project Framework helps us identify the next project to work on. The Benetech Truths define our culture and focus our efforts on how we operate.

BENETECH'S NEW PROJECT FRAMEWORK

We encounter examples of market failure in the technology field every week in our work. If a new product idea won't make tens or hundreds of millions of dollars, the technology business community is trained to put it on the shelf and move on to the next idea. It's hard to justify investing risk capital into markets that don't offer potential returns. For example, although human rights are a really important issue, the global market for software written to solve a specific problem unique to human rights is tiny: probably less than one million dollars a year.

Since Benetech has far more opportunities to respond to these gaps then we can take on, the goal of our new project process is to pick the one project each year that offers the greatest chance of making a difference. Here are our top seven considerations:

1. *Chance for revolutionary change.* If we can't revolutionize a field (for the better), it doesn't make sense to build a new software product. Making something 20 percent better than the status quo isn't enough. If we can lower the cost of delivering a social good (say, an accessible book to a blind person) by a factor of ten, or bring a technological capability to a community that didn't have a technology solution at all, now that's worth doing! So, our first issue is the social value proposition: why is this the best use of scarce resources in terms of return to humanity?

2. *User needs and product.* What are users doing today? Do we understand their needs? How will this new product thrill them and enable the social outcomes we (and they) desire? If we don't already have this knowledge in-house, do we know how and are we confident of getting it?

3. *Distribution and go-to-market plan.* Our product will only matter if we can get it to the people who need it. So many tech products are created; very few actually get to scale. Do we know how we will overcome the barriers to getting our product into user hands, and how we will ensure it's working well for users?

4. *Partnership plan.* Our products only make social change in the hands of others. Who will we need to engage to see that this happens? Also, Benetech doesn't want to staff up to do things that other people do better. Are there social enterprises we could be working with or through to accomplish our goal?

5. *Sustainability plan.* How will this social enterprise attain long-term sustainability? We generally need donors to invest in creating a new product and bring it to market, but after two–four years, will our donors not be needed because the product is sustaining itself on revenue?

6. *Exit options.* We're a technology company: in ten years, we shouldn't be doing what we're doing today. So, each new venture needs at least three exit options. One might be selling the venture to a for-profit company (we've done that once). Another might be spinning off a nonprofit, or having the technological problem we're solving be built into off-the-shelf mass market products.

7. *Low technical risk.* We assume we have plenty of technology available in the world. What's missing is the financial motivation to bring that technology to bear on social needs. We focus on execution in terms of the product and bringing it to the users, not creating risky new technology that hasn't been done before.

Each year, we look at the pipeline of dozens of good new project ideas and measure them on these. We choose a few ideas to develop further through more market research or creating a prototype. And then, we choose the one we think is the top contender. Don't worry about the other top ideas: a year later, almost all of them will still be waiting for someone to do them. That's the benefit of choosing unattractive markets; we don't have to elbow aside eager competitors!

THE BENETECH TRUTHS

Growth is challenging. How do you maintain the cohesiveness of a small mission-focused team as you add many people? As Benetech grew past 50 staff, we asked our team members what was true about Benetech. We very quickly came up with seven truths about Benetech, and we've since used these truths as touchstones for our decision-making. Whether it's picking a new project, or making a daily call on how to respond to a new problem, these truths set forth a cultural framework to help us decide what to do.

1. We are committed to social change through technology.
2. We get stuff done (not just theory and pilot projects).
3. We do the right stuff right (technically and ethically).
4. We prefer open to proprietary (open source and open content).
5. We think we can do more together (partnership).
6. We value flexibility.
7. We are committed to personal and professional development.

BOOKSHARE: AN EXAMPLE OF THE BENETECH APPROACH

Bookshare, our online library for people who are blind or have any other disability that affects reading, is a great example of the Benetech approach in action. We had just sold our Arkenstone reading machine product line to a for-profit company for roughly $5 million, a great example of a social enterprise exit option. We had to pick a couple of new projects in which to invest this funding, since as a nonprofit the money had to be committed to social good.

About that time, my son Jimmy (then 14 years old) had just installed Napster on our home personal computer. I was impressed with the power of the peer-to-peer approach, and with the questionable legality! And so the idea of Bookshare was conceived. We had forty thousand reading machine users, each of who used their scanners to turn inaccessible print books into text files that could be output with a voice synthesizer (or in large print with a printer, or in Braille with an embosser). What if they could share those scanned books with each other? A quick check with our attorney turned up the surprising fact that it was legal to do this under US copyright regulations!

The revolutionary idea was to blow up the traditional library serving the blind, which typically was able to do only 5 percent of the books needed by blind people. Instead of librarians making the difficult decision of which books to convert into audio cassette tapes or hardcopy Braille based on insufficient funding combined with high costs, people with disabilities would be in charge of the collection. If one person with a disability thought a book was worth scanning, we thought it would be worth sharing with tens or hundreds of thousands of other members of that community.

The cost per book added to the library would go down by at least a factor of ten (and in some cases, by as much as a factor of one hundred). And, if we could get to scale, we could see the same order of magnitude reduction in the cost of each book delivered, while hopefully solving 95 percent of the problem.

So, how did Bookshare measure up on our new project framework?

1. Chance to revolutionize the field: check.
2. User needs: we already understood those really well.
3. Distribution and go-to-market: a web-based platform should be doable.
4. Partnership plan: work with the user community to help create the library.
5. Sustainability plan: have our users pay modest subscription fees and eventually break even.
6. Exit options: sell out to the publishers once we'd demonstrated a market, or merge with one of the traditional libraries.
7. Low technical risk: we hired a couple of engineers who had built something similar more than once.

Bookshare also scored on our truths: it was social change through technology, we thought we could actually get it done, and we thought it was the right technical choice to make at the time (and it was legal!).

As a result, over less than ten years Bookshare has become the largest online library for the blind and print disabled communities in the world. Now, when a blind person needs a specific book for school, or work, or simply to read the same book as their peers without disabilities, the odds that title is in Bookshare is quite high. And, when the book is downloaded, the unit cost of delivering that book is now less than one-fifteenth of the traditional approaches.

Of course, not all went exactly according to plan. We thought that Bookshare would become viable on individual subscription revenue, which never reached a third of paying for Bookshare's then-modest budget. It turned out that meeting the needs of *students* with disabilities was the key to making Bookshare sustainable as it opened up the possibility of government funding; Bookshare now has more than 150,000 students. Also, after initial concerns from publishers about large-scale volunteer scanning of books, now more than 75 percent of the two thousand books added to Bookshare each month come voluntarily in high-quality digital form directly from leading publishers. So, our values of partnership and flexibility were in evidence as we shifted both where most of our books and our funding came from!

The Bookshare experiment took over six years to reach sustainability, but once there it succeeded in changing the field and expectations about solving the problem. We've built fresh partnerships, pioneered open source and open content solutions as part of Bookshare, and look forward to influencing the regular mainstream electronic book industry to directly sell accessible books to both people with disabilities and those without. Just one of the possible exit options we have in mind to solve this problem of accessible books for the long term!

Bookshare is just one example from the different social enterprises Benetech is operating today as well as the two new products we have in development. We've found that there are many, many opportunities for technologists to engage in social good. We've gone beyond thinking of our mission as simply building more and more products. Benetech wants to help catalyze the creation of many new organizations doing great things with technology. We hope to be part of a larger movement seeing that technology truly serves all of humanity, not just the richest and most able 10 percent!

Chapter 16

VAPOR TECHNOLOGY AND GIANT RATS

Bart Weetjens
Apopo

THE ROOTS OF APOPO BEGAN SPROUTING when I saw the dependence of African communities living in postconflict areas. There was a reliance on expensive imported know-how and technology to help rid their landscape of the destruction caused by landmines. It also lay in the unfairness of how we as a human society have evolved, and what we evolved into, with huge differences between the wealthy and the unfortunate. This is especially true when looking at the dependence of African communities on foreign input to create the most basic circumstances for development, which are simply not available. So in starting Apopo, I put myself in the situation of a subsistence farmer in an African village, unable to access his farmlands because they were filled with landmines. And I began looking at what these people had at hand and what resources could be utilized to tackle the problem of these buried landmines more independently. And since rats were plentiful everywhere, and I already knew that rodents had the capability, the idea of training them to smell the TNT in landmines and react to it became a solution to a very real problem. My intention, however, was not initially to train rats, but rather to deal with the dependency that had developed because of the existence of these landmines and empower these people.

My social commitment was something that had always been a part of my life. Being born in a middle-class Belgian family I had the experience of being in a world where nothing was lacking and where everything was possible. And yet at the same time, spending time in Africa and constantly seeing a miserable world—poverty really is an ugly monster with many heads—my direction almost defined itself. Empathy is very real for me and the skills developed through both my Buddhist and Christian values allowed me to commit socially. I think the third cornerstone that drove my work was having the good fortune to grow up in an extremely stimulating environment. My parents were both socially committed, both teachers, now retired. But they spent a life in service to community and taught me those values, which continued to inform and define my choices.

And, as most of us know, it is often in the most difficult circumstances that we come to the defining moments in our lives when our direction suddenly becomes obvious. It was no different for me. I had left university and started working in industry. I had several experiences in various industries for a couple of years, but nothing ever satisfied me. I didn't want to contribute to a system based on greed, depleting resources in a very linear fashion. I had always seen myself more as an artist. I met with a mentor of mine, Mic Billet, and after I explained my dilemma, he asked a simple question: "What kind of real world problem would you like to tackle?" There had been a great deal of press about the problem of landmines, and I had been giving it some thought; so I blurted out, "Landmines. It's not only a real problem, it's also a structural barrier to development." And in that moment, my new direction was clear.

Not too long after that, I was attending a conference in Edinburgh on new landmine detection technologies and I met a fellow product designer from Holland. We went out to a local pub and it turned out that he had a grant from the Dutch government to do exactly the same work I was doing—analyzing the landmine problem. And he was using the same design approach, with the same vision of appropriate technology that I had. It was a great encounter. As it turned out, he was at the end of his study, and was leaving all of it to go into architecture. And so right there in the pub, he handed his work over to me. And as I was going through it, I saw an article by Biederman and Weinstein, two scientists who had trained gerbils to detect explosives. They hadn't done so in a sustainable way—but it gave me evidence that rodents could smell explosives. And there was the total "aha" in that pub in Edinburgh. Having lived and worked in Africa I knew what they did have plenty of—rats.

I had already created a nonprofit that supported a school in Kenya, so I had a team on the ground, and had created a very small-scale organization. I was also lucky that one of the professors on my team became the vice chancellor of Antwerp University. He was well-connected with development corporations, and through his networks we actually got our first research grant to try and train rats to detect landmines. It is not a quick process and it requires a good deal of infrastructure and research, but we were able to launch the program and begin testing these ideas.

In assembling this project, I learned early on to install organizational procedures and managerial teams, and to let go of things. The second thing I learned was that I had to be adaptive. I've noticed that the same principles that apply in evolution theory apply to organizations, where whoever becomes rigid in their thinking or dogmatic is not going to survive. Especially within social and environmental nonprofits, people need to be adaptive to survive—it's not survival of the fittest, but of the most adaptive, which is the real meaning Darwin had in mind. That same principle applies in this context. It's a lesson I had to learn, to constantly and continually challenge our perception about all the resources we have around us—our human resources, our technologies, our animals, the environment, and all the environmental factors that we can respectfully use. But then it's not only challenging our perceptions, but—absolutely crucial—respectfully harmonizing with them. The fewer obstructions we create with our own opinions, the smoother the social change we are looking for can happen. Of course, within the social entrepreneurial world there is a lot of ego involved. Nowadays, we get all these accolades and recognition, but we have to be absolutely humble. There is no reason for us to claim ownership. It's the interdependence of phenomena that we have to see. And as soon the ego comes in, there will be trouble in the organization.

It's interesting to be working with animals, where it's not about ego. They have personality, but certainly not the ego attachment that we do.

We had chosen rats to work with because they were so plentiful and their weight wouldn't set-off the landmine. The problem, of course, was that there was an image issue that many in the African community and elsewhere have about rats. But there has been some compelling research done on rats by Prof. Jean Decety at Chicago University, in which he showed that rats can develop empathy. And what we found is that as we began working with these animals there was a love and connection that could be made with the animal, just as one might with a dog or a horse or a dolphin. People build an affective bond with these animals. I think that is partly why our training program was so successful—the trainers and rats were actually working together because they had created this bond.

As mentioned earlier, one of the obstacles we had to deal with was the image of rats. And in the early days especially, there were lots of difficulties with animal welfare organizations, and we even had one organization in New York publish a misinformed story that we were going to train suicide squads, kamikaze rat squads. But we have been able to overcome this by showing our care for the animals, creating the good circumstances we have for them to live in. They have toys and sufficient space, and we have outside pens for them. They are working animals, but they are very much taken care of, which is so essential in the program. There was also a lot of reluctance from the mine action community about using these rats to find the mines. But as it turns out, our training methods were incredibly effective, as were the rats. The rats have been so adept at recognizing smell that we've begun using them to detect other things—things you might never imagine, such as tuberculosis. And we're experiencing a similar reluctance from the medical establishment about using rats to detect TB in people. As one might expect, they are even harder to convince about the effectiveness of rats, even when we have quite compelling statistics. We've already demonstrated it works, with over twenty-five hundred people being detected to date.

Changing these perceptions takes a lot of research and very stringent experimental procedures, and then getting published in top journals. In the meantime, we're going on, bottom-up, saving lives and creating the circumstances for people to live better lives. We're not yet at the tipping point of acceptance, but we've reached a degree of sustainability, because as a social entrepreneurial effort, we are hired to bring our rats in and solve problems that devastate people and possibilities. We could do a lot more with additional funding and invariably have a greater impact. But that's not the main concern at this stage. Half of our income comes through operational contracts—and the other half comes from grants and donations.

At the same time, I don't think we've even scratched the surface of our full potential to tackle other social problems. We are continually looking for opportunities where our technology might make a difference. We have done experiments putting small video cameras on the backs of rats to search for survivors in collapsed buildings, and there are other commercial applications that could be very profitable as well. By looking for opportunities that could produce income, we can support our programs, which might not be fully self-sustaining. For example, one profit center we are currently looking into is the detection of tobacco. It would create a huge social impact to have a better grip on container transport of illicitly traded tobacco and contraband. These traffickers are off the radar, and the money that's generated here goes to some very unsavory activities such as human trafficking, arms trading, and all kinds of organized crime. We probably wouldn't do it under Apopo, as it is a not-for-profit organization, but under a separate structure where the profit generated would automatically be fed into the not-for-profit for humanitarian activities. The point is that if we don't limit our vision and imagination, new solutions emerge that can have a profound impact.

Of course, all of this requires teamwork, which is absolutely essential for success. To see possibilities and opportunities that are truly different and have an impact requires focus, leadership, and a willingness to change. Aspiring social entrepreneurs or social entrepreneurs in general need to understand that every time, in every moment, whatever difficulties we face, we have to weigh our choices against the values and cornerstones of our organization. If we can manage to make informed decisions related to these societal and environmental values that we hold, while at the same time letting go of our ego (i.e., the feeling that I have to do it all), then the unimaginable can happen. Rats can find landmines so that people can once again farm their land without fear for their lives and we can remove the dependency brought on by need. If we can operate from that place, it happens almost automatically.

Part 5

A HEALTHY ECONOMY REQUIRES A HEALTHY POPULATION

We know that a peaceful world cannot long exist, one-third rich and two-thirds hungry.

—Jimmy Carter

I would argue that a social justice approach should be central to medicine and utilized to be central to public health. This could be very simple: the well should take care of the sick.

—Paul Farmer

NONE OF US CAN OPERATE IN THIS WORLD when we are unable either to feed ourselves or keep ourselves well. A colleague of mine once told a group of us at a conference trying to find "Green" answers to our local economy, "A poor person doesn't give a damn about the environment when everything they do is about they're trying to feed and house their hungry family." That notion opened my eyes and touched me as few statements of fact I have ever previously heard. Before we can see to just about anything else, we all first see to our well-being and that of those we love.

The basics of food and health are often taken for granted by those of us who have it. For those who don't, it becomes all consuming. What makes these issues particularly insidious is that we live in a location where drought and access do not keep us from producing sufficient amounts of food to feed the population and we arguably have the finest and most respected health care facilities available to us. The mystery is that these issues continually plague us. The principle is simple—we all need food and access to health care. If the principle is correct, then the problem comes in the models we are constructing and the rules we've put in place to govern them as well as the attitudes and behaviors we hold toward those without.

One of my greatest inspirations, throughout the world of social enterprise, has come from Bill Shore. His notion, mentioned previously, of people who are doing this kind of work as seeing themselves as being cathedral builders puts everything into a greater perspective for me. And to have him be a part of this discussion and share what he has learned while running his Share Our Strength organization was one of the great thrills I've had in compiling this book. "Creating Good Work: The World's Leading Social Entrepreneurs Show How to Build a Healthy Economy" is what Bill Shore has spent his life doing for those who are hungry, for those who live without, and for those who, despite their lack, are a vital part of our society and need help. The system isn't working, and Bill offered another approach. Let those restaurateurs feeding those who can afford to dine elegantly help feed those who can't put food on their table at all. When I asked my friend and fabulous restaurateur Mary Sue Millikan, of Border Grill and Master Chef fame, if she would be willing to connect Billy and me, and when that positive reply came back from Billy, it was clear in my mind that the work at hand would be able to reach those affecting positive disruption at a level of head, heart, and soul. Billy's chapter is about how it gets done and done and done again, because we're all part of the process required for building the cathedral.

When I first saw Rebecca Onie accepting her Skoll Foundation Award a few years ago, I was taken by her work and dedication. As I looked more closely into what she was doing and how she was going about shifting decades' old perceptions of practice, held by those who often see themselves as infallible, medical doctors, I knew she needed to be represented in this discussion. Her social entrepreneurial effort, Health Leads, is not taking the old trodden path as being the only way to get from here to there.

She has simply stepped up and said our medical procedures are not helping people live healthier lives. The model needs to shift, as do the rules and behaviors we have held for ages. Health care is about creating healthy people, but that's not what our often overwhelmed health care systems have been delivering. The situation was not tolerable, and Rebecca did something about it, and she did so by hitting them, in among other places, directly in their prescription pads. The medical field has operated out of the "us helping them" mentality for centuries. What is now emerging is the understanding that we're in this healthy living cycle together. A doctor's charge is not merely to make us unsick, but to heal and help us all live healthy lives. Sometimes that requires something more than another pill. She is a shining example of what can happen when we apply the idea of deliberate disruptive design to a challenge. What emerges is a better answer.

Chapter 17

ACCESS TO A BETTER LIFE

Bill Shore
Share Our Strength

SHARE OUR STRENGTH WAS BUILT ON the belief that everyone has a strength to share; sometimes it's a gift that you may take for granted but that can be deployed to benefit others. Sharing strength goes beyond writing a check once you are financially successful or volunteering at a food bank or homeless shelter. Rather it means giving of yourself, of your unique value added, as chefs have done by cooking at food and wine benefits or by teaching nutrition and food budgeting skills to low-income families. In the same way we have engaged authors, architects, public relations and marketing executives, and numerous others.

Share Our Strength makes grants to a wide range of antihunger and antipoverty activities. I started the organization in 1984 with a $2,000 cash advance on my credit card and between that day and this we've raised and spent more than $350 million. We've organized more than ten thousand chefs and restaurateurs to participate in food and wine benefits, teach low-income families about nutrition and food budgeting, and to be a voice in the fight against hunger. And we've engaged thousands of corporate partners in cause-related marketing campaigns that create a new kind of community wealth.

Hunger is a problem, but it is a problem with a solution. In fact the extent of the problem has never been greater. According to Census Bureau Statistics, 48 million Americans live below the poverty line and 19 million of them live in deep poverty, families of four living on less than $11,500 a year. Also, 46 million are on food stamps and half of them are children. Secretary of Agriculture Tom Vilsack, whose department oversees child nutrition programs, says that one out of every two kids in this country will be on food assistance at some point in their lifetime. Today's generation of children faces hard times worse than anything since the Great Depression.

But the solution is as compelling as the challenge. For two reasons: First, children in America are not hungry because we lack food or food programs—we have both in abundance—but because they lack access to those programs. 20 million kids get a free school lunch but only 9 million get breakfast and only 3 million get meals in the summer when the schools are closed. Even though all 20 million are eligible. The reason they lack access is that sometimes they aren't aware of the program, but most times the state or city where they live hasn't set the program up.

Second, and this may be Washington D.C.'s best-kept billion-dollar secret, the food in the programs these kids lack access to is already paid for, its costs are 100 percent federally reimbursed. It buys milk from local dairy farmers, bread from local bakeries. But the money doesn't flow until the kids actually participate.

Here's the catch: These kids are not only vulnerable but voiceless. They don't belong to organizations and they don't have lobbyists. There is no greater testament to their voicelessness than the fact that $1 billion has been allocated for their needs and they are not getting it. These are federal entitlement programs but not the programs that have given entitlements a bad reputation. They are not drivers of the national debt. They represent the bipartisan wisdom of our predecessors, the wisdom that says kids are the most vulnerable and the least responsible for the situation in which they find themselves, and something as basic as whether or not they eat should not be subject to the prevailing political winds of the moment.

So what we do at Share Our Strength, in its very simplest terms, is work with governors and mayors, nonprofits and businesses, in public-private partnership, to identify the barriers to kids participating in programs like summer meals and school breakfast. And then we knock those barriers down. If it means working with community organizations to set up additional sites, that's what we do. If it means putting ads on radio stations to make parents aware of where their kids can get food, we do that too. Some recent results:

- Maryland: In 2010, there was a 45 percent increase in participation in summer meal programs over the previous year.
- Arkansas: They have nearly doubled the number of summer meals sites where families can access free summer meals.
- Colorado: There has been a 66 percent increase in the number of kids who are participating in school breakfast programs in 2010 and 2011.
- Washington State: There has been a 64 percent increase in participation in SNAP in Washington State.

In addition,

- Share Our Strength helped build the world's most sophisticated emergency food assistance network, guaranteeing that anyone hungry in America today has a place to go to get something to eat.
- Share Our Strength grants have meant the difference between life and death for tens of thousands of families in famine-struck nations such as Ethiopia and in developing nations such as Haiti, Guatemala, and Mexico.

What we are doing sounds good. But good is not good enough. Because Martin Luther King once said "In this unfolding conundrum of life and history there is such a thing as being too late. Procrastination is still the thief of time. The tide in the affairs of men does not remain at flood, it ebbs." Despite our success, there are still too many children for whom we are too late. The spectacular results we are getting in Arkansas have not found their way to Texas. The progress we've seen in Maryland has not reached Mississippi.

Like many nonprofits we face the task of solving the toughest problems of all: those that affect people so vulnerable and voiceless that there are no markets—no economic or political markets—available or dedicated to solving them. You don't see private corporations or public traded companies trying to do what Share Our Strength and other nonprofit partners in the fight against hunger are attempting. There is not a profitable market for it. Nonprofits exist to bridge that gap—to step in as a response to market failures. When those markets fail, we are first responders.

To define our strategy we thought about the writer Jonathan Kozol's advice to pick battles big enough to matter but small enough to win. This struck the right balance between inspiring but not completely out of reach. And so we refocused our broad-based antihunger efforts on a specific subset—hungry children in the United States—and realized it was possible to do more than just feed kids, that we could actually end childhood hunger. We pivoted from being the grant-making intermediary that we were for two decades, to designing and leading a national program committed to achieving specific, measurable goals toward an end to childhood hunger. This is what we learned:

1. *Go big or go home.* The linchpin of our growth was a commitment to shift away from short-term incremental progress in favor of long-term transformational change. The former is easy and comfortable. It is the norm, the natural order of things. You know how to get there. But so does everyone else. The latter is risky and hard to achieve. But it provides the inspiration that generates motivation, resources, and a new sense of what is possible. Chicago architect Daniel Burnham, who designed Washington D.C.'s Union Station, once said "Make no little plans. They have no magic to stir men's blood and probably themselves will not be realized. Think big." Establishing the bold goal of ending childhood hunger—not reducing, reversing, or redressing, but ending it—represented transformational change and more than any other factor has been responsible for our growth.

2. *Talent trumps all else.* Invest in talent first. Everything flows from it. Great ideas, great strategy, and great execution will not flow from a less-than-great team. Such talent is expensive and must be searched for in places that nonprofits do not always search. There are infinite rationalizations for not paying higher salaries, not replacing loyal but low-performing team members, not investing in seasoned managers

when you need them. Those rationalizations will save you money but they will not enable you to achieve your mission.

3. *Capacity equals impact.* Because nonprofits are not typically engaged in manufacturing, or supply chain, or warehousing, capacity usually means staff and technology as opposed to equipment, facilities, and so on. It is difficult to increase impact without increasing capacity. All of the incentives in the nonprofit sector run against long-term investments in capacity. As Clara Miller, founder of the Nonprofit Finance Fund, has explained: Philanthropy is enterprise blind and therefore enterprise unfriendly. All of the stakeholders of an organization—staff, board, donors, and beneficiaries—are so committed to creating social value everywhere and all the time that they favor investing in program instead of capacity and consequently, even if unintentionally, exploit the enterprise and ultimately hollow it out. Just as Warren Buffett has often explained that he always favors investing in building long-term competitive strengths over reaping short-term profit, organizational leadership must assert and defend the direct connection between capacity and impact.

4. *Accountability is a powerful differentiator in a crowded, competitive marketplace.* Good intentions have long been the Achilles' heel of the nonprofit universe because they are often the rationale for not being rigorous about measurement. But as the philanthropic marketplace gradually becomes more responsive and begins to reward high performance and superior strategy and execution and penalize low performance, stakeholders look for accountability. But accountability doesn't come cheap. It costs money to measure and to communicate what you've measured. That is money that might have gone instead into providing even more service or benefits to the population you serve. In the short term. But in the longer term accountability will eventually yield ever more resources so that you can serve more than you otherwise would have.

5. *Social entrepreneurship without public policy is like a garage band without amps.* It may be fun, cool, and trendy, but it won't reach very far. If your mission is ambitious and impactful the odds are it cannot be achieved without a public policy component. Building political

will simply means that you've succeeded in getting a broader base of people to care about your mission than just those immediately affected by it. There are many things nonprofits can do that the government cannot. They can innovate and take risks and be closer to the people they serve. But once they've built a better mousetrap, it requires public support to get it to scale.

6. *Most failures are failure of imagination.* As far back as the 1500s Michel De Montaigne wrote "Fortis imagination generat casum": a powerful imagination generates the event. Imagination makes it possible to envision and create a world that does not yet exist but is within our grasp. No one thought it realistic that college graduates without teaching degrees could succeed in underserved schools until Wendy Kopp and Teach For America imagined it. No one assumed that a pharmaceutical devoted to developing medicines for neglected diseases like malaria could operate as a nonprofit until Victoria Hale imagined it and created the Institute for One World health. At Share Our Strength our initial failure of imagination was to focus on feeding people not ending hunger. Once we made that leap everything changed.

The six principles listed here all contributed to our organization becoming more market-oriented and market-directed, leveraging the powerful market forces necessary to sustain and scale what works, and in some way compensating for the lack of natural markets that exists when working on behalf of those who are voiceless, vulnerable, and marginalized.

An African proverb says: "If you want to walk fast, walk alone. If you want to walk far, walk together." It has been our privilege, over the past 20 years, to bring thousands of citizens together to fight hunger. The collective efforts of these supporters are what enable us to walk far, to face the challenge of 48 million Americans living below the poverty line, of 17 million children who are at risk of going hungry in the richest nation on earth.

Each day offers more evidence that ending childhood hunger is possible. Children represent one of America's few areas of common ground. They hold appeal to Democrats and Republicans, liberal advocates and conservative corporations. In today's bitterly divided political climate, such common ground becomes sacred ground.

Chapter 18

WELLNESS IS MORE THAN NOT BEING SICK

Rebecca Onie
Health Leads

MY FRESHMAN YEAR, I signed up for an internship in the housing unit of Greater Boston Legal Services. I showed up the first day ready to make photocopies and coffee—but instead, I was assigned to a righteous and deeply inspired lawyer named Jeff Purcell, who thrust me on to the front lines right away.

Over the course of nine months, I had dozens of conversations with low-income families in Boston, who would typically come to us with housing issues, but when you scratched the surface, there was always an underlying health issue.

One of my clients was about to be evicted because he hadn't paid his rent—but he hadn't paid his rent because he was paying for his HIV medication, and he could not afford both.

A mother came in whose daughter had asthma but woke up covered in cockroaches every morning. One of our litigation strategies involved my going to the homes of these families and collecting the cockroaches in large glass bottles. I'd then hot glue gun them to a large piece of posterboard and take them to court. We'd always win because the judges reacted exactly how we expected, appalled. It was more effective than anything I learned in law school!

Increasingly, however, I grew frustrated that we were intervening so far downstream. By the time families came to us, they were inevitably in crisis.

At the end of my freshman year, I read an article about Dr. Barry Zuckerman, chair of pediatrics at Boston Medical Center, whose first hire as chairman was a legal services lawyer to represent patients.

With Dr. Zuckerman's blessing, in October 1995, I walked into the waiting room of the Boston Medical Center pediatrics clinic. The TV played an endless reel of cartoons, and the exhaustion of mothers who had taken two, three, and sometimes four buses to bring their children to the doctor was palpable.

Over the course of six months, I would corner doctors in the hallways and over lunch—asking them this naïve, but fundamental question: if you had unlimited resources, what is the one thing you would give your patients?

They said the same thing again and again; a story we have now heard hundreds of times:

> Every day we have patients who come into the clinic—their child has an ear infection and we give the family medicine, but the truth is, I know there's no food at home. The truth is, I know this family is living with 12 other people in 2 bedrooms and I don't even ask about those issues because there is nothing that I can do. I have 13 minutes with each patient, I have patients piling up in the waiting room, I don't know where to find food for them, and I have no help in doing so.

In that pediatrics clinic, even today, there are two social workers for twenty-four thousand patients.

HEALTH LEADS WAS BORN OF THESE CONVERSATIONS

In the clinics in which we operate, physicians can prescribe nutritious food, heat in the winter, and other basic resources their patients need to be healthy alongside prescriptions for medication. Patients then take those prescriptions to our desk in the clinic waiting room, where our corps of well-trained college-student advocates "fill" those prescriptions by work-ing side-by-side with the patients to access the existing landscape of com-munity resources.

We began with a card table in the clinic waiting room—lemonade stand style. Last year, our corps of one thousand college volunteers worked to connect nearly nine thousand patients and their families with the basic resources they need in 21 clinics.

Eighteen months ago, however, I received an email that changed my life. It was from Dr. Jack Geiger—who wrote enthusiastically, in his words, "to share a historical precedent" for Health Leads.

This is the story he told: In 1965, Dr. Geiger founded one of the first two community health centers in the United States in a desperately poor area of the Mississippi Delta. So many of his clients presented with malnutrition that he began writing prescriptions for food. Patients could take these to the local supermarket, which would fill the prescriptions and charge the clinic pharmacy budget.

When the Office of Economic Opportunity, which was funding Geiger's clinic, found out, they were furious—and sent down a bureaucrat to inform Geiger that they expected their dollars to be used for medical care. To which Geiger famously and logically replied: "The last time I checked my textbooks, the specific therapy for malnutrition was food."

I knew when I got that email that I should be proud to be part of this history. But the truth is, I wasn't proud. I was devastated.

Here we are, 45 years after Geiger prescribed food for his patients, and I have doctors telling me: on those issues we practice a don't-ask, don't-tell policy; 45 years after Geiger, Health Leads had to reinvent the prescription for basic resources.

One of the key challenges we face at Health Leads is ensuring that we do not reinvent the wheel—or worse yet, end up in a situation 45 years from now when another bright-eyed college student walks into the clinic wait-ing room and comes up with the same idea. We know what we need to do to have a *health* care system, rather than a *sick*care system—so why don't we do it?

This is the hard question facing Health Leads, and it requires us to be honest with ourselves. My belief is that it is almost too painful to name out loud our aspiration for our health care system, so long unarticulated—or to even admit we have one at all: because, if we did, that aspiration would seem desperately remote from where we are now.

Health care, like any other system, is just a set of choices people make. What if *we* decided to make different choices, to make this system what it was meant to be?

That's what we have begun to do at Health Leads: We started with the prescription pad and its purpose and asked not what do patients need to *get* healthy, but rather, what do they need in order to *be* healthy, to not get sick in the first place. The change came from asking new questions of this powerful piece of paper. In this case, we didn't just accept the prescription as we have always done it.

In many instances, there are several types of challenges that an organization like Health Leads faces: (1) the behavioral, (2) the operational, and (3) the systemic. The first has to do with the very tangible question of implementing something you know works—such as the prescription pad—and determining how it can be seamlessly integrated into a diverse set of partner clinics with different patient flows, physical layouts, staffing compositions, and reimbursement structures.

When changing behavior, know the benefit of that behavior change is not always enough. Helping those who you want to implement change means they need to understand why the change is needed and why things are intolerable without it. When this need is clear, behaviors can change.

At Children's National Medical Center, one of our partner institutions, every time a patients show up for primary care appointments, they're now asked a few questions about basic resource needs: "Are you running out of food at the end of the month? Do you live in safe housing?" So when the doctor begins the visit, she knows: height, weight, is there enough food, is the patient living in a shelter.

This informs a different set of clinical decisions, *and* the doctors can prescribe these resources for their patients, making Health Leads like any other subspecialty referral.

If we could empower individual doctors to prescribe food and heat to their patients, then the next challenge is to change the operating presumption of a whole hospital.

Operationally, changes require small shifts in procedures as to how things are done. At Harlem Hospital Center, for example, every time a patient comes in with an elevated body mass index, the electronic medical record automatically generates a prescription for Health Leads, and our corps of college-student advocates then works with the patient to access healthy food and exercise programs—a presumption that if you're a patient at that hospital with elevated BMI, the usual clinical care in the four walls of the doctor's office probably won't be sufficient; you likely need more.

On the one hand, this is just a simple recoding of the electronic medical record. On the other hand, that recoding shifts the EMR from a mere repository of diagnostic and treatment information, to a live health promotion tool.

In the private sector, when you squeeze this kind of additional value out of a fixed-cost investment, it's called a billion-dollar business. But in Health Leads's world, it's called less obesity and reduced diabetes. It's called *health care*—a system where doctors can prescribe solutions to improve health, not just manage disease.

Last, there is the challenge of systemic change. Health Leads has taken on the work of developing a compelling case that the health care system should pay for basic resource connections. Understanding that health care is what health care pays for, we believe that services like Health Leads's will not become a systematic part of health care delivery until the economic value of addressing patients' resource needs is demonstrated. Our goal is that by 2015, 20 percent of our total budget will be from earned revenue, defined as hospitals, third-party payers (insurers), or health departments paying for the services that Health Leads provides. There are three core reasons that we are interested in securing earned revenue from our clinic partners: first, as with any social enterprise, Health Leads is eager to build out its revenue model and reduce its risk of reliance on philanthropy alone. A true earned revenue model would be a major catalyst for the organization, and also enable future growth and longevity. Second, the presence of an investment from our clinics signals a true partnership: institutions are more inclined to act as thought partners and join us in ensuring programmatic success as well as clinical integration. Finally, we believe that in order for resource needs to become integral to the health care system, this work must be financially integrated into hospitals; operating budgets.

With health care dollars tightening, the ability to secure earned revenue that will be a major driver of our work—and the vision is that it could ultimately result in a health care system—is regularly reimbursing resource connections.

Health Leads is fortunate to have an extraordinary community of philanthropic supporters that assist the organization in moving along its trajectory while also unpacking complicated questions such as that of the business case. In 2011, Health Leads completed an $11.1 million "proof fund" campaign, which has provided the organization with the unique ability to innovate, adapt to ongoing learning within the organization, and prepare for the unexpected. While our vision for changing the health care system to include resource connections as a standard part of patient care may be ultimately unachievable, the proof fund enables us to take risks that few others in our field are unable to. Organizations in the nonprofit sector often find themselves faced with the challenge of setting a destination (i.e., a comprehensive growth strategy) before they've had a chance to construct the pathway to get there—and then must raise money toward that static destination.

The beauty of the proof fund is that it is a significant investment in the pathway itself—and acknowledges that organizations such as Health Leads can achieve highest impact when they are given space to test, retest, and recast hypotheses. The impact of our proof fund has been twofold: it has enabled us both to make traction on our strategic plan while simultaneously providing us with a core group of 16 investors that serve as extraordinary thought partners and advisors to the organization. These investors explicitly invested in a high-risk/high-return premise—and the result is that they are often as deeply embedded in our success as our own internal team—helping us with talent sourcing, connecting us with external consultants, and generally catalyzing our organizational development. The proof fund has enabled us to exercise great flexibility and thoughtfulness in the way that we achieve our ultimate vision of a health care system that addresses all patients' basic resource needs as a standard part of quality care.

Part 6

SOCIAL JUSTICE: THE PEACEFUL WARRIOR'S QUEST TO CREATE A SANER WORLD

If we live our lives according to a principle of selflessness, placing others first, then we can actually lead others—for we can discover how we can fully unfold their own wisdom and basic goodness.

— Sakyong Mipham Rinpoche, Dechen Chöling (2003),
unedited transcript

INJUSTICE SERVES NO ONE, and yet it exists throughout all levels of society and in almost every nation on earth. It shows up as social inequities, psychological neglect, racial exclusion and oppression, torture and physical abuse, and unfortunately the list goes on far too long. It is one of the most painful of social challenges social entrepreneurs address because it is inflicted on people by other people, and the scars it leaves rarely heal. The spectrum of offense takes injustice from the most insidious of actions humans execute against each other, to the unconscious ignorance that results from benign neglect. Social injustices are the most difficult of areas for us humans to look directly at and admit it can be done, it is being done, and that by our inaction we allow it to be done.

This is not an issue that gets raised in polite company because it is so impolite, and yet seemingly so tolerated. It is easy to be against social injustice, and because of its prevalence, obviously very easy to perpetrate. In many instances, it is easier to raise awareness about animal abuse than it is about the abuse of humans. And it continues, while you read this, in darkened and well-lit corners, in cities, suburbs, rural areas, and in virtually every language spoken. Fortunately, there are those who say "enough." There are those who recognize that the victims of injustice usually are those who can't protect themselves, who can't defend themselves, and those who have the weakest voices among us.

In fighting for social justice Karen Tse has been at the forefront of ending the torture of prisoners around the world. Her organization, International Bridges to Justice (IBJ), is an extraordinary example of what can be accomplished when one person's vision is made collective. Karen's actualization of her deliberate disruptive design is intelligent, fearless, compassionate, and forgiving, in the best sense of what that means, as a way of ending behavior that is not only debase, but inhuman. The accolades Karen has received are well deserved and her dedication is inspiring and motivating. How she steps up and meets the activities of people, acting toward others at their very worst, is not only courageous, it is transforming. It is difficult to separate Karen's story from how she has made her organization work and helped stop the useless practice of torture around the world, but the lessons contained in her chapter should be emblazoned on the credo of every social entrepreneurial effort—even when we don't want to open our eyes to what is in front of us, we must be fearless and forgiving, and, nonetheless, in doing so, be unrelenting in putting an end to the often unconscionable and negative behavior we encounter.

When singer Peter Gabriel launched WITNESS.org in 1992, he too recognized that the way to rid ourselves of the social injustice we find is to place a large spotlight on it until it shrivels up beneath the exposure. One thing that seems to unite people, at least theoretically, is that inhumanity is intolerable. Putting an end to it starts with action, followed closely on its heels by more and more and louder communication. Often those victims of social injustice have no means of letting others know of their plight. WITNESS began by putting cameras into the hands of those ordinary folks with the weakest voice and yet one of the most powerful messages on earth. These were people subjected to injustice, all over the world. What Gabriel knew from his work with Reverend Desmond Tutu is that it didn't have to be like this. Tutu and Nelson Mandela were part of a society for which injustice was endemic. But when they finally overthrew their oppressors, when they had the opportunity to retaliate and pay back the atrocities perpetrated upon them, they chose not to, but rather to shed a searing light on the problem and move forward without repeating the offense. The actions of these two individuals and their colleagues was undoubtedly one of the greatest achievements of the twentieth century. The work WITNESS has now done for over 20 years is to make injustice visible. No matter how hard it is to look at its face, here is a video of it and this is the compelling story we must tell to make it stop.

These two organizations are examples of what can be done to shift what seems unshiftable. How they make this work and the lessons they share are applicable in any social entrepreneurial effort in which "enough" has become the calling.

Chapter 19

ENDING TORTURE, NOW

Karen Tse
International Bridges to Justice

MY JOURNEY TO BECOMING A SOCIAL ENTREPRENEUR began in 1994 when I walked into a prison in Cambodia and met a 12-year-old boy who had been tortured and denied access to counsel. I looked into his eyes and realized that although I had written hundreds of letters for political prisoners, I would never have written a letter for him. He was not a 12-year-old boy who had "done" something important for anybody; he was not a political prisoner; he was a 12-year-old boy who had stolen a bicycle. What I also realized at that point was that this didn't happen only in Cambodia. This type of abuse is widespread in many countries. Every day in countries throughout the world people are detained, tortured, and denied access to counsel. Most of the victims are ordinary people, too poor to hire a lawyer to protect their rights. This abuse, I also realized, is 100 percent preventable because the majority of these same countries have passed laws to protect their citizen rights. However, they lack the international support and resources for proper implementation. Because of this awakening, in 2000 I founded International Bridges to Justice (IBJ) and began to organize, train, and support networks of defenders worldwide to undertake the work of ending torture and implementing due process rights.

BUILD COMMUNITY IN PURSUIT OF SHARED VALUES AND VISION

The ideal of justice requires bridging the gap between one's inner life and values and one's work in the outer world. This core principle of IBJ—of finding common ground through shared values—manifested itself practically when I was working with police in Cambodia, to try to get them to discontinue their recently outlawed practice of torturing suspects. I designed a workshop that started with basic questions that connected them to some of their values and hopes for the future. I began by asking the police why they had decided to become police officers in the first place. Most of them said that they had become police officers because they wanted democracy. They pointed to the atrocities of the Khmer Rouge and talked about how they didn't want to ever go back to a period like that again. Yet, they also said that they were vehemently against the new laws, which stated that there was a "presumption of innocence" for prisoners who had not yet received a fair trial. They also stated that they felt torture was the only way to get prisoners to "tell the truth" and confess to the crime that they had just committed. I introduced the notion that these confessions were perhaps not very reliable, but many insisted that tortured confessions were reliable. I brought in a picture of the posted rules of the former Khmer Rouge ToulSleng torture center. The posted rules, which ironically underscored the presumption of innocence, stated: "Don't you dare try and tell a lie or you will be given more lashes."

The officers began to consider all those thousands of people, including their relatives, who gave confessions under duress and torture. "This, the old system, is a system where presumption of guilt is operating," I said. "Do you really agree with this system?" The officers began to look again at their values and beliefs. They spoke about how they wanted to move forward from their past and not move backward. Over some time, many began to reconsider whether the "old" way of doing things was really the right way. And because of their reflection, many decided that they wanted to change and did. They did this together, supporting each other in community. Today IBJ has taken this model of training based on the reflection of core values from Rwanda to India to China. Our training programs not only focus on legal skills and concepts, but also are based on the premise that in order to truly affect change in communities people must reconnect to their own inner values and build community in pursuit of shared values and vision.

BELIEVE IN THE POWER OF TRANSFORMATIVE LOVE

While I am a lawyer by training, the grounding principles of IBJ are not only based in law, but also on spiritual values and a sense of shared humanity. Too often people think that solving the world's problems is based on conquering the earth, rather than touching the earth, touching the ground. I learned to touch the ground in my human rights work many years ago, and since then spirituality, which had not previously been a part of my work or approach, became the basis of what I do.

This approach is in large part due to some profound advice I received regarding my human rights work when I was working as a human rights lawyer in Cambodia almost 20 years ago. During a moment of crisis, I had sought advice from Sister Rose, an Indian nun from Mother Teresa's order. She ran the Missionaries of Charity orphanage where I volunteered in my spare time. The chief of the police force with whom I was conducting training sessions regarding their practice of torture had been making veiled threats on my life. It was deeply troubling; my ability to continue working was in question. I asked her a simple question, "What should I do?" After a moment of thought, her answer, too, was simple: "You must seek to find the Christ in each person, or you must seek to find the Buddha in each person. Then you must work with that Christ or Buddha." Like my meditation teacher who had offered me similar advice, she believed in the power of transformative love.

The power of transformative love opened up new visions and new horizons of possibility and hope to me. Building upon what I had discovered spiritually while at Harvard Divinity School, I realized that it was human beings, not their laws or institutions or a pure reliance on divinity, that created history. In many countries torture had become part of the accepted culture. But a culture that is built by humans can be changed by humans. Although human-created legal foundations were in place to protect the accused, they clearly weren't sufficient. We needed to take the next big concrete step, to implement these laws—to make them part of a new reality.

I believe that all humans were created to bring about a more peaceful and just society. This human action, this spiritual dimension of seeing humans as cocreators, was missing from the puzzle to end torture.

COMBINE THE PRACTICAL AND THE DARING

This approach and vision has impelled us to work with all sorts of actors at all levels and to operate upon a principle of interconnectedness. For example, we have signed memoranda of understanding with the governments of China and Zimbabwe out of our vision that there is always common ground to be found. This approach to preventing torture is both principled and pragmatic. We're trespassing into prophetic imagination through our top-down, bottom-up approach. We work together with governments and players in the criminal justice system, not against them, and educate even those who might otherwise engage in torture, such as the police. We also train ordinary citizens in rights awareness, protect grassroots movements, and empower people from the bottom up. We work country by country, providing direct legal assistance to the accused, building dialogue within the justice sector, and educating citizens about their fundamental rights. But we also work globally, building online training materials and resources for defenders across the globe and creating links to bring about a worldwide movement. This combination of the practical and the daring, leveraging both top- and bottom-level actors, generates the dynamic energy that is vital to our success.

We're working to build a global movement that creates a shift in what is perceived as acceptable. At one time slavery was an accepted practice. Now the world recognizes how wrong it is. We want to create the same global shift in consciousness with respect to torture. We are a small NGO; we can't address every injustice in every corner of the world all at once. But our goal is to shift consciousness and make torturing the accused unacceptable. Then the norms will change. To do this, we combine our legal and pragmatic programming foundations with the spiritual. We have faith to step into the unknown, trespass into prophetic imagination, and be innovative enough with our legal and pragmatic methodologies, while trusting that our overriding vision is possible. We move forward in faith even when the evidence is to the contrary, because we believe in the unknown possibilities.

All along the way, I had to make compromises with myself to start and continue the journey because I was a reluctant entrepreneur who lacked the inclination for running an organization. At first, I said to myself, "Listen, you don't like running organizations. You don't want to run an organization, but clearly there's a need for this in this world. Therefore, what you can do is start the organization, put the infrastructure in place, create the Mission Statement, secure funding for it and then you can retire after a year." That *actually* was my initial negotiation with myself. I accepted that compromise and told myself I'd do it for one year. But then there was no funding, so I negotiated with myself to pursue it for another year, and then another, and another. It's now twelve years and I'm still here. And I've just successfully negotiated another twelve-year contract with myself to put all the systems in place to end torture as an investigative tool and implement due process rights by the year 2024. Of course, in the middle of this quest it is rarely easy. Attaining our vision will continue to be challenging until people truly believe that it is possible to end torture as an investigative tool and implement due process rights and are committed to it as a core value. Sometimes we fall down, but we always get back up and always keep moving forward. How do we keep our operations moving forward during challenging times? We have found that it is necessary to always be creative in the way we utilize our resources in order to make our vision a reality. We remain flexible and innovative. In addition, in order to reach scale, we know we must create a tipping point throughout the world if we are going to effectively end the use of torture as an investigative tool and implement due process rights. To achieve this, we have to optimize all of our technological resources and networks. For example, we have created e-learning programs through which we reach people throughout the world that we normally would not be able to serve. We have created a "Wikipedia-like" website as a resource for our defenders working on cases throughout the world. Our JusticeMakers program enables us to bring our mission to new places and inspires enthusiastic lawyers from many different countries to make a difference. To date, we have supported 34 JusticeMakers in 26 different countries. This program not only creates a global community for defenders who are otherwise extremely isolated and unable to collaborate together, but the program also funds defenders each year who are committed to advocating positive reforms in their respective countries. This program attracts very talented and resourceful individuals who might not otherwise have the opportunity to implement effective, innovative, and sustainable reforms. Furthermore, these technological resources allow us to connect and unite our defenders in a common mission, giving them hope, and reminding them in the middle of their hardships and difficulties that they are not alone. This has a ripple effect.

The perseverance of defenders in these challenging situations is remarkable. In Zimbabwe, five of the prisoners we had worked with died in custody. I remember going to Zimbabwe and hearing our two lawyers there say, "You know it's a difficult situation, but come to the prison." I came in to the prison and the lawyers said, "The food situation is bad. Prisoners receive one meal a day, but everyday they choose 30% of them to give it to because there's not enough food." I went in and I saw the distressing situation. As I stood before them I asked some of the prisoners, "How long have you been here for pretrial detention?" They answered: five, eight, or even nine years. We were very discouraged as we walked out of the prison and realized that we had nowhere near the resources needed to help all the prisoners. We decided to organize a workshop to enlist pro bono lawyers to our cause. During that workshop, there was a break during which one of our lawyers heard some of the participants commenting on the impossibility of the task. When we returned from the break he gave an impassioned speech to continue believing we could make a difference. He said, "The lack of resources is never an excuse for injustice." And with this, he successfully organized a team of pro bono lawyers who have since worked tirelessly in taking on hundreds of cases. They have made a real difference in thousands of lives. It's a tremendous program, so we struggle to continue it however possible even though at present it is completely unfunded. Yet, despite such hardships, the courage of the defenders we work with continues as they find creative ways to cobble together even small resources and move toward a vision of the future, despite all the obstacles before them. As they move forward in difficult times, despite the outward circumstances they face, they still have hope. And because they have hope, I have hope. We all hold on to the hope that it is possible to end torture as an investigative tool and implement due process rights in our lifetime. And it is this hope that moves us to action. Together, let us move forward from fear to hope.

Chapter 20

VIDEO ADVOCACY AT THE LEADING EDGE OF HUMAN RIGHTS

Jenny Coco Chang
Witness

THE IDEA FOR WHAT WOULD BECOME WITNESS emerged from a very personal experience of singer Peter Gabriel, back in the late 1980s. He had gone on an international world tour with Amnesty International, and carried with him a Hi8 camera, the state of the art at the time, so he could capture and film the stories people were sharing of imprisonment, torture, and violence. He realized then that if people could meet and hear the stories that he was hearing, it would be hard for them to deny these things were taking place, and they would be moved to act to right these wrongs. Peter recognized, even then, the power of the visual image to create change.

Then in March of 1991, the Rodney King incident took place in Los Angeles, California, and the world watched in shock at the video proof of police officers overreacting to a situation and helplessly beating a man lying on the ground. When those officers were acquitted of the charges that they had used excessive force, it sparked national outrage, a riot in the streets of Los Angeles, and, ultimately, sparked a dialogue about racism in America. It was not until the footage of the Rodney King incident became widely distributed that funders really understood what Peter Gabriel already knew—visual images can catalyze discussion, understanding, and create change.

But where did that video of Rodney King being beaten come from? It came from a bystander named George Holliday, who happened to have a camera, was at the wrong place at the right time, and caught it all on video. He then shared it with the media.

Peter's vision had inspired the birth of WITNESS. And when The Lawyer's Committee for Human Rights (now Human Rights First) and the Reebok Human Rights Foundation joined forces with Peter and provided the seed money to launch the program, WITNESS became a reality, in 1992.

Today, and for the last 20 years, WITNESS has focused its work on empowering people to transform their personal stories of abuse into powerful tools for justice, as a means of promoting policy change through public engagement.

Human rights work is based on personal values. Our funders, and for that matter, everyone who is involved with WITNESS, is here because they personally believe in and have a deep desire to stop human rights abuses wherever they are occurring. They also know that video is an incredibly powerful tool and vehicle to be able to accomplish that objective.

To give you just one brief example, one of my colleagues and a good friend, Bukeni Waruzi, who is now WITNESS's program manager for Africa and the Middle East regions, had previously served as executive director of one of our partners, AJEDI-Ka. This is an organization that works on the issue of child soldiers in the Democratic Republic of Congo. While he was with AJEDI-Ka, he spent several years documenting the stories of child soldiers that were forced to be in the army of former rebel leader Thomas Lubanga Dyilo. Bukeni produced several videos about these children, one of them called "A Duty to Protect." This film was eventually submitted to the International Criminal Court (ICC) as evidence against Lubanga. The video explored the complexity of the war, the issues confronted by girl soldiers, including rape and sexual exploitation, and the critical importance that the ICC end the rampant impunity reigning in the Eastern DRC. In 2005, Lubanga was arrested, and in 2009, the ICC began its first ever trial focused on child soldiers. Then on March 14, 2012, the ICC found Lubanga guilty of using children in armed conflict—a war crime. The ICC judge said at the end of the trial, "[U]nable to dispute visual images and deny the sound, the video evidences presented to us were credible and outstanding."

ADAPTING TO THE NEED

When he founded WITNESS, Peter's goal was to distribute video cameras to human rights activists on the ground, so they could document human rights abuses. We soon realized that it wasn't enough to just distribute cameras—our partners needed both technical training in how to use the cameras, and, most importantly, strategic training in using video as part of a campaign to create change. What that meant was teaching people how to get these videos in front of people who can make a difference.

Since this became our model, WITNESS has trained hundreds of human rights activists in 80 countries to use video as a tool in their human rights campaigning. We call this "video advocacy."

Today, technological advances have caught up with Peter's original vision to give video cameras to the world. The use of mobile phones has proliferated at astounding rates across socioeconomic, geographic, and cultural boundaries, revolutionizing the way we interact with each other. This offers the potential for anyone, anywhere, to become a human rights defender and a video maker. Capturing evidence of abuse has never been easier. In some ways, Peter's vision has become a reality.

The challenges we face today are still many. Finding forums or places to share footage of those abuses and finding the online tools to create context for the footage is an ongoing challenge for grassroots activists and the growing number of citizen activists that are turning to video to demand social change in their countries. We need look no further for evidence of this than to the Arab Spring and Syrian uprisings and the dramatic footage coming out of these events.

But now that cameras are everywhere, we are finding there are unintended consequences that human rights defenders and WITNESS hadn't counted on. Safety and security issues are now on the rise. Activists in Syria, for example, are risking their lives to share with the world, through media and social media, the recordings of killings, abuses, and atrocities happening at the hands of the Syrian security forces, as an appeal for the international community's help. However, as their pleas are being distributed, their identities are also being collected by the Syrian authorities, who are now using facial recognition technology to target activists and track them down.

Today, the focus of WITNESS's work is shifting to deal with these challenges by looking for opportunities to use video and existing digital technology more safely, securely, and effectively for anyone who wants to turn to video to defend human rights.

We are building digital tools that will help blur people's faces. We are putting all our training resources online, from basic camera work training to strategy on messaging and distribution. We are also making those resources available in different languages and actively engaging with commercial technology companies to find new opportunities in which they can make their products more beneficial to human rights defenders. For example, after working with Google for many months, we were able to launch a Human Rights Channel on their YouTube platform. This is a place where activists that are uploading their videos on YouTube can alert us to the existence of the footage; we can then work to verify the authenticity of that video with our partner, Storyful. Once we have that authentication, we begin distributing it to the media and the public.

FLEXIBLE YET FOCUSED

The process of getting to the point where our work and films are now respected around the world was not always a linear pursuit. We were established in 1992, but we didn't actually have a fulltime executive director until 1998, when Gillian Caldwell came on board. WITNESS also didn't become incorporated until 2001 when we had a staff of only four people. In those early years, WITNESS relied on established foundations within our founding organizations to move forward with our work and mission.

The year 2005, however, was a turning point for WITNESS. The Omidyar Network gave us a $1.7 million grant over three years, which allowed us to scale up and shift from being a small organization operating with limited resource to a larger one, with more employees and a new office space. This too had unintended consequences. It turns out that it was challenging for an organization to shift from a grassroots-like operation to one that runs as an organization in which there are suddenly many new people now responsible for running various programs and projects.

In the early years, WITNESS was often equated as Peter Gabriel and Gillian Caldwell's project. Today, WITNESS is known as a human rights organization that uses video advocacy to advance human rights campaigns. WITNESS = WITNESS. Nonetheless, Gillian Caldwell and Peter Gabriel are still very much a part of the organization, although they are no longer at the center of every project.

One of our greatest internal cultural adjustments was to be able to shift our leadership from a top-down approach to one in which leadership was exhibited throughout the staff. Today, everyone in the organization has to undergo a leadership course and build their own leadership skills around the areas for which they are responsible.

It was also important for us to become more transparent within our organization, which included relationships with staff. This was a conscious effort to do things a bit differently than other organizations. At WITNESS, the executive team makes presentations to the staff. For example, the organization's budget, priorities, and goals are all presented to the staff, not as a way of simply sharing the information, but also to get feedback and buy-in from the staff as to the direction in which we as an organization will be traveling. We recognize that that alignment is central to our moving forward.

DEVELOPING AND CONTINUING THE WORK

From a funding perspective, we get support from a mixture of foundations, major gifts from individuals and family foundations, and our annual gala. Currently, about 41 percent comes from foundations, but we are finding that we have reached the limit on those resources, having tapped into all the foundations that fund organizations involved in human rights. Now, we are focusing on securing more major gifts, which currently provide only about 16 percent of our funding.

On a practical level, we are always researching and reaching out toward new opportunities for funding, through personal introductions, via email, social media, and through events. The fact is that our supporters love physically meeting us and coming to our work space. They like seeing where we work, how we work, and who is doing the work. In making the trip to our offices, however, they are always quite impressed by how small our space actually is. We seem so big because we are able to do so much. That is a trait that runs through the entire organization, and is really a reflection of the personality of every single staff member. We know we are doing work that needs to be done, and there is a lot to do.

We are also an organization that has a very diverse staff. There are people working here from all over the world. On our staff we have people who speak Spanish, Portuguese, French, Swahili, Turkish, Chinese, Russian, Arabic, and that just names a few. We are also a staff made up of a lot of young people, volunteers, and interns. So there are always young and fresh ideas flowing through the organization. It is also imperative that we are nimble and flexible, able to shift gears if we need to. That is both a characteristic and strength of our organization. Many of our staff members are fearless in what they are willing to try as well as the issues they are willing to confront. If an idea seems good and there is something we feel should be done, it doesn't usually take long for us to get behind it and get it off the ground.

The challenge is always one of sustaining new ideas, as well as finding the funds to continue what we have built. Our reputation has been built on empowering people on the ground and balancing that with the human resources we need to develop new tools. In addition, we now manage a Human Rights Channel and must continue to engage with technology companies, who are considered the new human rights players, so that we can continue to work together to develop tools that better serve the human rights community.

Our vision, today, is far greater than when we started our efforts, and trying to juggle it all with a staff of 30 and a $5 million budget requires ingenuity and dedication; but I think it's clear, we are getting there.

ONWARD

Ron Garan
Astronaut/Manna Energy Foundation

IN JUNE OF 2008, I CLAMPED MY FEET to the end of the robotic arm (Canadarm-2) on the International Space Station. With me in this position, the arm was flown through a maneuver we called the "windshield wiper," which took me across a long arc above the space station and back. At the top of this arc, I was 100 feet above the space station looking down at this incredible accomplishment of humanity against the backdrop of our indescribably beautiful Earth, 240 miles below. Seeing the absolute beauty of the planet we have been given was a very moving experience. But as I looked down at this beautiful, fragile oasis—this island that protects all life from the harshness of space—I couldn't help but think of the inequity that exists. The people who don't have clean water to drink, enough food to eat, and the social injustice, conflicts, and poverty that exists. When we see our Earth from the orbital perspective, we are struck by an undeniably sobering contradiction. On the one hand, we see the absolute beauty of our planet, and on the other, there are the unfortunate realities of life on this planet that affect a significant portion of her inhabitants.

I returned to Earth after that first space mission with a call to action. I could no longer accept the status quo on our planet. We have the resources and technology to solve many, if not all, of the problems facing our planet, yet nearly a billion people do not have access to clean water, countless go to bed hungry every night, and many die from preventable and curable diseases. We live in a world where the possibilities are limited only by our imagination and our will to act. It is within our power to eliminate the suffering and poverty that exist on our planet.

On my second space mission, I spent half of 2011 living and working onboard the International Space Station. I spent most of my free time gazing back at our Earth wondering what the world would be like in the next 50 years and pondering the question, "If we have the resources and the technology to solve the challenges we face, why do they still remain?"

I believe that the answer to why our world still faces so many critical problems, in spite of our ample technology and resources, lies primarily in our inability to effectively collaborate on a global scale. Although there are millions of organizations around the world working to improve life on Earth, for the most part, these organizations are not engaged in a unified, coordinated effort. There is a great deal of duplication of effort, loss of efficiency, and unfortunately, in many cases, unhealthy competition.

We have the technology that can enable true global collaboration that is world changing. Our real challenge, as social entrepreneurs, is demonstrating how vital and valuable collaboration is, despite the real and perceived risks. It is the only real way to enable economies—and solutions—of scale. Perhaps most importantly, collaboration encourages greater accountability and fosters trust.

There has to be a way for all of us involved in social entrepreneurial efforts to collaborate toward our common goals. An effective collaboration mechanism would pair together challenges with solutions. It would bring together unique pieces of the puzzle and enable us to learn from each other's successes and failures while making us far more effective than we would be otherwise. There are a variety of organizations developing tools to enable collaboration. It is critical to unify these efforts as well.

As I looked back at our Earth from orbit, I saw a world where natural and man-made boundaries disappeared. I saw a world becoming more and more interconnected and collaborative, where the exponential increase in technology was making the impossible possible on a daily basis.

Thinking about the next 50 years, I imagine a world where people and organizations work together toward their common goals. They set aside their differences and realize that each and every one of us is riding through the universe together on this spaceship we call Earth. And because we are all interconnected, we are all in this together and, therefore, the only way to solve the problems we all face is together.

I can imagine a world where open/transparent collaborations become the engines that fuel tremendous economic growth and help us overcome many of the problems facing our planet. It's a world in which those individuals and organizations that engage in unhealthy competition, secretive dealings, and corruption see themselves being left behind and having to adapt, evolve, and take on a much more effective collaborative mindset in order to keep up with the economic growth that collaboration will bring. I can imagine a world where we all firmly believe that by working together we can accomplish anything. Can you?

For most of our human history, the vast majority of people believed that it was impossible to fly to the Moon—simply because it had never been done before. Human ingenuity and the determination of the human spirit proved that it was possible. Today, many people believe that it is impossible to solve many of the social problems of the world. It is widely believed that is impossible to lift the entire global population out of poverty. "There have always been poor in the world and there always will be," they say. If we can land on the Moon and return to Earth safely, if nations can join together and build an enormous research facility in orbit, then by working together we can solve the challenges facing our planet—including the alleviation of poverty. Nothing is impossible.

The first step to affect change is to believe that real change is possible. If we all commit to work together, I believe that in the next 50 years it is possible to live in a world without poverty, where no one dies from preventable and curable diseases, where everyone has access to clean water and no one goes to sleep hungry, in a world that educates all its children. I believe that we are presently living in a world where the possibilities are endless, and where we are limited only by our imagination and our will to act. You don't have to be in orbit to have the orbital perspective. By working together, we do not have to accept the status quo about the challenges we face on our planet. Act together. We are not alone here.

APPENDIX: APPLIED WISDOM AND LESSONS LEARNED

DESIGNING ENTERPRISES TO DELIBERATELY disrupt how social challenges are addressed and ultimately solved is a task that demands a tremendous amount of research, planning, and strategic thought. Launching a social enterprise solely because it's the right thing to do—while certainly noble and worthy—is something akin to charging off to deal with a dragon and knowing nothing about dragons. The result should be obvious: You and your efforts will surely end up as toast.

A couple of years back, Archbishop Desmond Tutu addressed the congregation of the Skoll World Forum, nine hundred ardent believers in the pursuit of social entrepreneurship. Tutu, speaking from his own extraordinary accomplishments, reminded the assembled that we cannot undertake this work we wish to do, alone. He told a story about a light bulb, which no matter how bright it can shine when it is screwed in and turned on, is useless when it rests next to the lamp. "We all stand on the shoulders of others," he told the group. But he then added something that pierced the hearts of those who work so tirelessly on these pursuits. He said pointing directly at those in the audience, "But it is you—what you do validates God." To me what he was saying was that our work validates the basic goodness that is our inherent nature as humans. When social entrepreneurs are tasked with a responsibility like that, there is no denying that we are often led by our hearts rather than our heads. Bishop Tutu's benediction, however, was not about increasing the egos of those in the auditorium, but acknowledging the drive and the intention, which is both blessing and curse.

Social entrepreneurs must also remember what Jeff Trexler reminded us: that as social entrepreneurs, we must be willing to apply the idea of deliberate disruptive design to ourselves just as we do to the social challenges we confront. We can make change happen, but we can only do so when we combine what is in our hearts with the knowledge that is in our heads.

The social entrepreneurs who have offered their insight, experience, and expertise in this book have provided a collective wisdom for this rapidly expanding workforce trying to shift the unshifting. It is something that has never been collected in this fashion before. It is a generous gift from those who have felt a similar calling to this work, and concluded it was imperative to share what they know. For this reason, we have made an effort here to collect, in a highly condensed form, some of the wisdom, lessons, and expertise about which you have just read. This listing is not intended to be something akin to a social entrepreneurial declaration of best practices. Best practices are useless, in and of themselves, because they are invariably situational. But when adapted, reshaped, and applied locally to each individual situation, it means we don't have to start from scratch every time. These lessons can also serve as a map of the territory others have traveled. But the map, of course, is not the territory. The landscape changes, the players change, and the interactions initiated are always different, as are the new opportunities that emerge. But by adapting what others have learned and putting these applications into practice, perhaps, one day, we can solve the social challenges we encounter, and put all of our efforts out of business—which, by the way, should be the exit strategy of every social entrepreneur.

ESTABLISHING THE VISION

Push the frontier where others have yet to tread. We innovate to reach a broader range of families who live in poverty, including farmers who grow staple crops for domestic consumption rather than high-value cash crops for export.

Think big. The key to understanding poverty alleviation is the quotation from BRAC's founder, Sir Fazle Hasan Abed: "Small may be beautiful, but big is sometimes necessary."

Passion and commitment will carry you a long way. If you can't project confidence and a firm belief in the rightness of your idea, no one else will "buy it."

Capitol alone is often not enough. We have seen that capital alone is often not enough to unlock businesses' potential for growing prosperity.

Big institutions don't like taking risks, which is where you as the entrepreneur enter. Large firms, organizations, and governments have been around so long that staff sometimes confuse longevity with always doing the same thing the same way. Entrepreneurs invent continuously and relentlessly.

Study the system, the landscape, and the community around you. Build community. Recognize what is missing, but also envision what could be there and contribute to filling the gaps. Strong relationships are essential to any endeavor.

Keep the momentum going. Keep learning and listening from your colleagues and allies—the community will support you if you are attuned to their needs.

Changing perceptions takes a lot of research and very stringent experimental procedures. In the meantime, keep going on. For us, that means continuing to save lives and create the circumstances for people to live better lives.

Believe in the power of transformative love. Grounding principles can be based on spiritual values and a sense of shared humanity.

Shift consciousness but be willing to make compromises. Work to build a global movement that creates a shift in what is perceived as acceptable.

Visual images can create change. Sometimes that means that people are in the wrong place at the right time.

Be fearless in what you are willing to try as well as the issues you are willing to confront. If an idea seems good and something should be done, it won't take long to get people behind it and get it off the ground.

CREATING THE ORGANIZATIONAL CULTURE

We have learned that it is much easier to teach the hard skills than to teach passion, intuition, empathy, or values. The hardest part of building an organization is attracting, training, and retaining talent.

The importance of culture is critical in an organization seeking to have impact at scale. It represents a common thread and an opportunity to celebrate our work as a team.

You will likely encounter very hard times; build up your resistance. Whether you need to ask staff to skip payroll (possibly during the holidays) or invest your own time and money, times will be rougher than you expect, change will take longer than you plan. Build up your support system—family, friends, colleagues, advisers—you will need them!

Beware of overborrowing. Caution is necessary to avoid overindebtedness, which is counterproductive to the social goals of microlending.

Monitor, evaluate, adapt, perfect, and scale up. Accounting on the field level is monitored by a team of internal evaluators, and the organization holds to a zero tolerance policy if it encounters corruption among its ranks.

If you are building an organization for the long term, diversify. Depending on a single source—public, private, or your relatives—is dangerous to your enterprise's long-term health.

Find a unique niche, and work it. It may be lonely out there—in fact, it should be, if it is yours and yours alone. But keep at it—as long as you can keep your ultimate goal in sight.

Find key partners to support you in areas you are weaker. Focus on your strengths and gifts, delegate and partner on the rest.

Eliminate cultural obstacles to implementation. Make sure your organization assesses others' capacity to use your services well to ensure that there's rapid buy-in of the services.

Keep the faith, implement improvements wherever you are. Sometimes the timing and team is not yet ready. You could be 1, 5, or 10 years ahead of when the timing is right. If you happen to be too early, find a landing spot that can help you wait it out, and practice your skills and build your own expertise.

DO NOT REINVENT THE WHEEL

A culture that is built by humans can be changed by humans. All humans were created to bring about a more peaceful and just society. This spiritual dimension of seeing humans as cocreators has been missing from the puzzle to end torture.

Shift leadership from top-down to one in which leadership is exhibited throughout the staff. Provide everyone in the organization leadership training and build their leadership skills around the areas for which they are responsible.

Alignment is central to moving forward. The more transparent an organization can be, the greater the feedback and buy-in from staff to move together toward the direction in which the organization will be traveling.

Build a federation not a franchise. The difference is that a franchise says that there is a model that you can replicate. With a federation, you have things that you share and gain from each other, but there is not a one-size-fits-all model.

Be aware of the generational when starting-up a new model. Older generations, especially the ones with the resources to support the vision, may not understand it from their older workforce paradigm.

There needs to be demand for the product or else you will not be in business. Weave social mission into competitive advantage so that the better you do at the business, the more impact you are making as a social enterprise.

ACTUALIZING THE PROCESS

First, understand the market, the key customer segment, and the essence of the business model. Attend events across a variety of sectors where disruption is occurring in order to understand the region and its relationship to social innovation.

Increase risk tolerance to move things forward. Understand the notion of fail fast, and the idea of making decisions based on milestones versus going back and forth about a particular decision.

Sometimes we struggle and that's good. We need creativity and flexibility to attack the problems we attempt to fix, yet we need the structure that will help us all collectively achieve our goals.

Break the silos across sectors and industries with multidisciplinary solutions. All innovation comes from the intersection of two or more specialties that had not met before. So, take one or more human, social, and ecological needs, add in a business approach that generates financial sustainability, and a new social enterprise could be born and flourish.

Pilots should be rigorously tested to assess the viability of new products and ventures. Do this before they are launched nationwide

Embrace the power of convening. Create events for community building in your target area.

Enjoy the process. Burnout is not an option. Keep it fun easy and inspiring.

Keep the balance and quality of life on the radar screen. Take care of your body, emotions, and spirit.

Listen twice as much as you talk. You have two ears and one mouth, so remember that ratio. It will also help if you hear twice as much—from customers, employees, stakeholders, investors and donors, and society.

Learn to trust others with your dream. Lead from a distance and watch and respond to emotions when unexpected problems occur. Trust begins by trusting oneself. Building trust with those with whom you interact virtually starts with you.

Be adaptive. The same principles that apply in evolution theory apply to organizations: whoever becomes rigid or dogmatic in their thinking is not going to survive. Especially within social and environmental nonprofits, people need to be adaptive—it's not survival of the fittest, but of the most adaptive. Teach people how to get in front of people who can make a difference and look for opportunities.

Be nimble and flexible—able to shift gears when needed. It can be challenging for an organization to shift from a grassroots sole proprietor operation to one that runs as an organization in which there are suddenly many new people now responsible for running various programs and projects.

Change comes from asking new questions. Don't just accept what is known to be the only way.

Innovate and adapt to ongoing learning within the organization. Trust the wisdom of the team—the whole team.

Bridge the gap between one's inner life and values and one's work in the outer world. Find common ground and build community in pursuit of shared values and vision; then train based on the reflection of core values.

Combine the practical and the daring. Leverage both top- and bottom-level actors to generate dynamic energy.

Pay it forward, and cultivate the next generation. Whatever age you are, you can always invest in others who can help. We are all in this together—and running in the same direction with force and speed can help build a better world faster than any of us can do alone!

Prepare for the unexpected. Because it will happen.

DEVELOPING RESOURCES AND FINANCE

Develop a growing and financially sustainable portfolio. At an aggregate level, a growing and financially sustainable portfolio enables an organization to demonstrate the financial and impact opportunity while attracting capital from investors and inspiring replication by peers and partners.

In lending, aim for impact, scale, and financial sustainability. This creates a demonstration effect that attracts new capital from existing and new financiers to serve those that cannot be reached by an organization. Do so in a way that promotes sustainable social and environmental practices.

Build equity in your enterprise, in the form of net worth. It validates your track record, gives you credibility, makes your "next big idea" more plausible. Not to mention the fact that it gives you "staying power" and resilience when hard times come, as they inevitably will.

Constantly and continually challenge perception about all resources. Challenge human resources, technologies, the environment and all the environmental factors that can respectfully be used. It's not only challenging perceptions, but—absolutely crucial—respectfully harmonizing with them—letting that dialog go between our inner and outer worlds, while remaining true to our values. The fewer obstructions we create with our own opinions, the smoother the social change we are looking for can happen. It's a question of allowing it to happen.

Always be creative in the way you utilize resources. Optimize all technological resources and networks.

Always research and reach out toward new opportunities for funding. Utilize personal introductions and communicate via email, social media, and through events.

REACHING THE GOAL

There's nothing better than reaching your big goal. But celebrate small triumphs along the way.

CONTRIBUTORS

Alan R. Andreasen is professor of marketing at Georgetown University. He is a world leader in the application of marketing to nonprofit organizations, social marketing, and the market problems of disadvantaged consumers. He is the author or editor of 18 books (including revisions), numerous monographs, over 135 articles, book chapters, and conference papers. He has advised, carried out research, and conducted executive seminars for the World Bank, American Cancer Society, AARP, USAID, CDC, American Red Cross, United Way of America, Boys and Girls Clubs of America, and public health programs in the developing world. He is board member of Gifts in Kind International. He was awarded the 2007 Richard W. Pollay Prize for Intellectual Excellence in Research on Marketing in the Public Interest and, in 2008, the first lifetime achievement award of the Marketing and Society Special Interest Group of the American Marketing Association.

Allen R. Bromberger is a partner at the New York City law firm of Perlman & Perlman. He holds a BA from the University of California/Berkeley (1977) and a JD from the University of California/Hastings College of the Law (1982). Mr. Bromberger has more than 30 years of experience structuring a wide variety of for-profit and nonprofit social ventures, nonprofit/for-profit joint ventures, commercial coventures, and substantial nonprofit earned revenue ventures. Mr. Bromberger has participated in numerous business and academic meetings and panels on the development of the fourth sector and the legal issues involved in creating socially responsible and "hybrid" business ventures. He is a member of the board of directors of the American Sustainable Business Council and the Fourth Sector Network, and serves as legal advisor to the Catherine B. Reynolds Program on Social Enterprise at New York University.

Jenny Coco Chang has over 14 years of media and strategic communications experience for progressive issues and organizations. As a broadcast journalist, she has worked for a number of international media outlets, including Young Asia Television in Sri Lanka, Media Corporation of Singapore, and STAR-TV in Hong Kong. As an independent producer, Coco produced documentaries for CNN Asia, National Geographic Channel, and World Wildlife Fund. As a communications strategist, she played a critical role in helping the PBS Foundation raise over $20 million dollars for programming and services that benefited 356 public television stations across the country. Coco has also developed effective communications and new/traditional media outreach strategies for a number of progressive organizations to enhance campaign efforts on issues such as animal rights, human rights, national education, public health care, social and economic justice, urban homelessness, and women's rights. Coco has a master's in International Policy and Practice from George Washington University and a master's in Public Communications from American University.

Susan Davis is a founder and current president and CEO of BRAC USA in New York. She was a founding board member and chair of the Grameen Foundation. She has led Ashoka's Global Academy for Social Entrepreneurship and cofounded the University Network for Social Entrepreneurship. Ms. Davis serves on Ashoka's international board committee and is a senior advisor to New York University's Reynolds program on social entrepreneurship and coauthored *Social Entrepreneurship: What Everyone Needs to Know* with David Bornstein.

Craig P. Dunn is associate dean and director of Graduate Programs within the College of Business and Economics at Western Washington University and an associate professor emeritus of San Diego State University, in both instances specializing in business and society issues. His research interests include managerial ethics and values, corporate social responsibility, corporate governance, the meaning of work, and social entrepreneurship. He is active in the International Association for Business and Society, publisher of the journal *Business & Society*—serving as a fellow. He has served on the board of directors of Mission Federal Credit Union, the Greater Golden Hill Community Development Corporation, the Corporate Governance Institute, the Green Restaurant Association, Lydia Place, as well as the Ethics Advisory Panel for the Institute for Local Government, the research arm of the League of California Cities, and the Ethics Advisory Committee of the Port of Bellingham. Craig is a senior consultant with the Centre for Organization Effectiveness.

Glenda H. Eoyang, PhD, is a master teacher with deep insights into the art and science of self-organizing systems. As a pioneer in the field of human systems dynamics, Eoyang applies principles of self-organizing to help people thrive in unpredictable environments. As the founder of the field of human systems dynamics, she brings a strong and cogent voice to public discussions about the field. She currently serves as founding executive director of the Human Systems Dynamics Institute, a network of professionals working at the intersection of complexity and social sciences. Her published works include three books: *Coping with Chaos: Seven Simple Tools*, *Facilitating Organization Change: Lessons from Complexity Science*, and *Voices from the Field: An Introduction to Human Systems Dynamics*, an edited collection of practitioner stories that demonstrates the transformative power of systems dynamics.

William Foote is founder and CEO of Root Capital. He began his career as a financial analyst in the Latin American Corporate Finance group at Lehman Brothers. Early in his career, he worked as a journalist in Mexico and Argentina where he discovered the challenges faced by cooperatives and small producers who lacked access to credit and markets. He founded Root Capital in 1999 (originally EcoLogic Finance). William was named a Skoll Fellow in 2005, an Ashoka Global Fellow in 2007, a Young Global Leader by the World Economic Forum in 2008, a member of the Young Presidents' Organization (YPO) in 2009, and one of Forbes' "Impact 30" in 2011. He is on the executive committee of the Aspen Institute's Aspen Network for Development Entrepreneurs (ANDE) and is a life member of the Council on Foreign Relations. He currently serves on the boards of

E&Co, LASPAU: Academic and Professional Programs for the Americas, and the Open Learning Exchange (OLE). William holds an MS in Development Economics from the London School of Economics and a BA from Yale University.

Carrie Freeman has been studying and collaborating on how business can be a key contributor in an ever-advancing civilization for nearly 20 years and strongly believes that it is the purpose and responsibility of business to improve society. Prior to recently joining SecondMuse, Carrie worked for Intel Corporation as the director of Sustainable Business Innovation. A strong advocate for using information and communication technologies to help solve global challenges, she was responsible for developing the vision and business opportunities for Intel's technology solutions in the areas of environment and natural resource management. Additionally, she developed other innovative strategies such as a corporate impact investing fund that targeted financial, social, as well as business strategic returns. As the corporate sustainability strategist, Carrie helped form the corporate sustainability group and directed corporate-wide sustainability efforts working with internal and external stakeholders to ensure industry leadership. Carrie regularly speaks around the world on the role of technology and sustainability, innovation, and corporate responsibility. She has collaborated with corporations, multilateral and development organizations, industry consortia, nonprofits, and academia on sustainability initiatives. Passionate about expanding human potential, Carrie is a certified performance coach and has trained hundreds of individuals. She is on the boards of the Nature Conservancy of New Mexico and the Permaculture Credit Union and acts in an advisory capacity to the Water Innovations Alliance and the Technology Venture Corporation.

Jim Fruchterman is a leading social entrepreneur and CEO of Benetech, a nonprofit technology company based in Palo Alto, California. He is a former rocket scientist who creates technology social enterprises that target underserved communities. In 1989, Fruchterman founded Benetech, a nonprofit social enterprise, to produce reading machines for people who are blind. Benetech now creates new technology for people with disabilities as well as the human rights and environmental movements. Fruchterman has received a MacArthur Fellowship and the Skoll Award for Social Entrepreneurship. He believes that technology can be the ultimate leveler, allowing disadvantaged people to achieve more equality in society.

Ron Garan is presently working in NASA's Open Government Initiative, which seeks to develop innovative collaborations within government, industry, and with citizens around the world. He recently returned from a six-month mission of scientific research and exploration aboard the International Space Station. One of his personal objectives during the mission was to use the unique orbital perspective to put a focus on the challenges facing our planet. Ron has a strong belief in the ability of social entrepreneurship and appropriately targeted philanthropy to solve many of the problems we face here on Earth.

R. Paul Herman is the founder and CEO of HIP Investor Inc., a wealth manager and investment adviser to individuals, families, family offices, and foundations. The HIP Scorecard, which quantifies impact and relates it to financial value, is described in detail in Paul's first book—*The HIP Investor: Make Bigger Profits by Building a Better World* (John Wiley & Sons, 2010). R. Paul Herman is a registered representative of HIP Investor Inc. in the states of California, Washington, and Illinois—any investment information is not a recommendation, and past performance is not indicative of future results. Learn more about Paul, how HIP helps investors build a better world through their portfolios, and the HIP book at www. HIPinvestor.com.

Michael Karlberg is the author of *Beyond the Culture of Contest: From Adversarialism to Mutualism in an Age of Interdependence*, as well as numerous journal articles and book chapters on related themes. He assisted with the development of the Harmony Equity Group's founding conceptual framework and has since served as a consultant for SecondMuse as it seeks to advance a process of systematic learning within that framework. He is also a professor of communication at Western Washington University.

Todd Khozein works with SecondMuse, a consultancy specializing in the use of collaborative processes to conceive and incubate innovative initiatives. He personally focuses on studying and applying the emerging science of collaboration. His interests lie in the incubation of collaborative frameworks where the incentive structure, technological platform, and human resource development initiatives align to create a culture of innovation. Todd holds a BA in Economics and a doctor of medicine degree from the University of New Mexico.

Gary Kosman is the founder & CEO of America Learns, a firm that works with nonprofit and social justice organizations worldwide to track and expand their impact. Gary was named among the ten best emerging social entrepreneurs worldwide by Echoing Green, the global social venture firm. In September 2007, former president Bill Clinton recognized Gary and America Learns in the book, *Giving: How Each of Us Can Change the World*. Gary also received an iParenting Media "Excellent Products" award for his coauthorship of the parenting book *Bonding While Learning: Activities to Grow Your Relationship While Preparing for Reading Success*. In his spare time, Gary volunteers with the Network For Teaching Entrepreneurship, hikes, skateboards, and reads. He's currently working with his mom to start a new company in the food industry.

Rebecca Onie cofounded Health Leads (formerly Project HEALTH) in 1996, as a sophomore at Harvard College, along with Dr. Barry Zuckerman at Boston Medical Center. From 1997 to 2000, Rebecca served as executive director of Health Leads. In 2006, Rebecca returned as chief executive officer of Health Leads, now operating in Baltimore, Boston, Chicago, New York, Providence, and Washington, D.C. Last year, Health Leads' corps of nearly 1,000 college volunteers assisted 8,800 low-income patients and their families in accessing food, heat, and other basic resources they need to be healthy. In 2009, Rebecca was honored to receive a MacArthur "Genius" Fellowship. In 2010, O! Magazine named her to its power list of 20 women who are "changing the world for the better." Most recently, she was named to Forbes Magazine's Impact 30, recognizing the world's top 30 social entrepreneurs. Rebecca is a World Economic Forum Young Global Leader, US Ashoka Fellow, and member of the Young Presidents' Organization and the Mayo Clinic Center for Innovation External Advisory Council. She has received the John F. Kennedy New Frontier Award, the Jane Rainie Opel '50 Young Alumna Award, and the Do Something Brick Award for Community Leadership.

Clifford Rosenthal served for more than 30 years as chief executive officer of the National Federation of Community Development Credit Unions, the association for financial cooperatives that serve low-income and minority communities. He authored the concept paper that laid the foundation for the federal Community Development Financial Institutions Fund, and served as the first elected chairman of the CDFI Coalition. Trained as a Russian historian, he is the coauthor and translator of *Five Sisters: Women against the Tsar*. He has received the highest national awards of the US credit union movement, the Opportunity Finance Network, the Insight Center for Community Economic Development, and other national and New York City organizations. In recognition of his work in raising funds for community revitalization after Hurricane Katrina, the ASI Federal Credit Union in New Orleans named its community center in the Upper Ninth Ward after him. He holds bachelor's and master's degrees from Columbia University in New York. In May 2012, he accepted a position leading the Office of Financial Empowerment of the newly created Consumer Financial Protection Bureau in Washington, DC.

Ron Schultz is founder and president of Entrepreneurs4Change. The enterprise works with green and social businesses, veterans, and marginalized communities, providing entrepreneurial education, access to funding and capital, and ongoing nurturing and support for the businesses once they are operating. He also founded Volunteers of America, Los Angeles' Social Entrepreneur Incubator. He has written as well as coauthored several books. His last book, *Coherence in the Midst of Complexity*, written with Hugo Letiche and Michael Lissack, was published in January 2012. His other books include *Adjacent Opportunities–Sparking Emergent Social Action* (2010), *Unconventional Wisdom* (1994), *Open Boundaries: Creating Business Innovation through Complexity* (with Howard Sherman, 1998), and *The Mindful Corporation: Liberating the Human Spirit at Work (with Paul Nakai, 2000).*

Bill Shore is the founder and chief executive officer of Share Our Strength®, a national nonprofit that is working to end childhood hunger in America, raising and investing more than $315 million in the fight against hunger. He has won the support of national leaders, from governors and mayors to Oscar-winning actor Jeff Bridges. Share Our Strength's No Kid Hungry® campaign is ending childhood hunger by connecting kids to the healthy food they need, every day. Shore is also the chairman of Community Wealth Ventures®, Inc., a for-profit subsidary of Share Our Strength that offers strategy and implementation services to foundations and nonprofit organizations. Shore was named in America's Best Leaders by *US News and World Report* and has received many prestigious awards including the Jefferson Award for Greatest Public Service by a Private Citizen. He is the author of four books focused on social change, including *The Cathedral Within* and his most recent book, *The Imaginations of Unreasonable Men*, the story of the great imagination and spirit possessed by great social entrepreneurs. A native of Pittsburgh, PA, Shore earned his BA at the University of Pennsylvania and his law degree from George Washington University in Washington, D.C.

Dorothy Stoneman is founder and CEO of YouthBuild USA, Inc., the national support center for more than 273 YouthBuild programs in the United States, and 56 in 12 other countries including Mexico, South Africa, and Israel. In YouthBuild programs, low-income, unemployed youth ages 16–24 who lack a high-school diploma enroll full time for 6–24 months. They work toward their GED or diploma while building affordable housing for homeless and low-income people. A caring adult staff emphasizes personal responsibility, mutual support, and leadership development. Graduates go on to jobs in the construction industry or to college. Many earn AmeriCorps education awards for their service in the community. Since 1994, more than 120,000 YouthBuild students have produced 22,000 units of low-income housing in America's poorest communities. Stoneman has a bachelor's degree from Harvard University and master's and doctoral degrees from Bank Street College of Education. She was awarded the international Skoll Award for Social Entrepreneurship in 2007–2013, the John Gardner Leadership Award in 2000, and a MacArthur Fellowship in 1996. She has worked in the fields of youth and community development since 1964.

Jeff Trexler is president of Second Tree Ventures and teaches fashion ethics, sustainability, and development for the Fashion Law Institute at

Fordham Law School. Prior to this, he was professor of social entrepreneurship at Pace University and taught nonprofit organization law at Saint Louis University, SMU School of Law, and the Yale Law School.

Karen Tse founded International Bridges of Justice (IBJ) in 2000 to promote systemic global change in the administration of criminal justice. A former public defender, Karen first developed her interest in the cross-section of criminal law and human rights as a Thomas J. Watson Fellow in 1986, after observing Southeast Asian refugees detained in a local prison without trial; thousands of prisoners of all ages being held without trial, often having been tortured into making so-called confessions. In 1994, she moved to Cambodia to train the country's first core group of public defenders and subsequently served as a UN judicial mentor. Under the auspices of the United Nations, she trained judges and prosecutors, and established the first arraignment court in Cambodia. In the initial stages, she negotiated groundbreaking measures in judicial reform with the Chinese, Vietnamese, and Cambodian governments. Under her leadership, IBJ has expanded its programming to include Rwanda, Burundi, Zimbabwe, and India. In addition to the Defenders Resource Centers in those countries, IBJ also sponsors independent Justice Makers in 25 countries. IBJ has created a Global Defense Support Program to bring IBJ assistance to public defenders worldwide. In 2010, IBJ launched the Justice Training Center in Singapore. A graduate of UCLA Law School and Harvard Divinity School, Karen was named by US News & World Report as one of America's Best Leaders in 2007. She has been recognized by the Skoll Foundation, Ashoka, and Echoing Green as a leading social entrepreneur. Karen was the recipient of the 2008 Harvard Divinity School's First Decade Award, and the 2008 American Bar Association's International Human Rights Award. She also received the 2009 Gleitsman International Award at the Harvard Kennedy School of Government.

Bart Weetjens is a celebrated social entrepreneur. He trains HeroRATs to save human lives from disaster and disease. Bart addressed the dependence of African communities on foreign expertise to solve difficult, dangerous, and expensive humanitarian detection tasks posed by scourges of the developing world, like the landmine legacy and the emergence of tuberculosis. His organization APOPO researches, develops, deploys, and disseminates the use of a sustainable local alternative: detection rats technology. HeroRATs are humanely trained giant African pouched rats that act as cost-efficient detectors in limited resources settings, while building local expertise. Bart is an Ashoka fellow, a Skoll awardee, and a Schwab fellow to the World Economic Forum. Bart is a Zen Buddhist priest. He lives with his wife and two daughters in Tanzania.

Greg Wendt is a veteran financial advisor and certified financial planner, and is considered a thought leader in the field of sustainable and responsible investing. Since 1991, he has advised clients who want to align their wealth through investments that reflect their priorities and concerns for a better world. He built his expertise while working with major Wall Street firms such as Smith Barney, UBS Paine Webber, and Prudential Securities. Currently Gregory is vice president of Sustainable and Responsible Investing at EP Wealth Advisors, Inc. Greg is founder of two nonprofit efforts—Green Business Networking and Green Economy Think Tank. He is a member of the California Financial Opportunities Roundtable, a select group of experts convened by the Federal Reserve Bank of San Francisco and the USDA Economic Development to address the financial needs of communities in California.

CONTRIBUTORS' WEBSITES

America Learns: http://americanlearns.net

Apopo: www.apopo.org

Benetech: www.benetech.org

BRAC USA: www.bracusa.org

Echoing Green Foundation: www.echoinggreen.org

Entrepreneurs4Change: www.e4c.net

Green Economy Think Tank: www.greeneconomythinktank.org

Health Leads: www.healthleadsusa.org

HipInvestor: www.hipinvestor.com

Human Systems Dynamic Institute: www.hsdinstitute.org

International Bridges to Justice: www.ibj.org

Manna Energy Foundation: www.mannaenergy.org

McDonough School of Business, Georgetown University: http://msb
.georgetown.edu

National Federation of Community Development Credit Unions: www
.natfed.org

Perlman and Perlman: http://www.perlmanandperlman.com

Root Capital: www.rootcapital.org

Second Tree Ventures: http://www.secondtreeventures.com

SecondMuse: www.secondmuse.com

Share Our Strength: www.strength.org

Western Washington University: www.wwu.edu

WITNESS: www.witness.org

YouthBuild: http://youthbuild.org

To view videos of the social entrepreneurial contributors in the application section of this book, go to the social action media network—www.samnet .tv—and enter the username CWG and the password code CGW.

INDEX

Printed in the United States of America